THE SEA BIRD

THE SEA BIRD

Rozelle Raynes

SPRINGWOOD BOOKS

© *Rozelle Raynes 1979*

Printed in Great Britain by
Latimer Trend & Company Ltd, Plymouth
for Springwood Books Ltd
Bedford Row, London
ISBN 0 9059 4777 0

For Dick
who taught me the folly
of single-handed sailing

A wind's in the heart of me, a fire's in my heels,
I am tired of brick and stone and rumbling wagon-wheels;

I hunger for the sea's edge, the limits of the land,
Where the wild old Atlantic is shouting on the sand.

From 'A Wanderer's Song'
by John Masefield

CONTENTS

1	*The Call of the Sea*	*1*
2	*A Boat of my Own*	*17*
3	*To Sea in a Sieve*	*30*
4	*Single-handed Passage*	*46*
5	*Shipwreck*	*58*
6	*I Learn to Sail*	*66*
7	*Sailing to Russia*	*81*
8	*A Night to Remember*	*114*
9	*Another Kind of Sailing*	*119*
10	*I Join the Merchant Navy*	*130*
11	*Ferry Me to France*	*158*
12	*The Road to the Stars*	*183*

ILLUSTRATIONS

BETWEEN *pp.* *100/101*

1 Sue, Winkle and author as Wrens on naval pinnace
2 Author scrubbing decks—Nieuport, Belgium
3 Author working on *Imp* in winter quarters in Dover
4 *Imp* and author being towed past the Hurlingham Yacht Club
5 A busy day in the Pool of London. *Photo:* Fox Photos
6 My cousin Gillian Maude—sailing into Ostende
7 Bernard, Alexandre and Robert aboard *Souer Thérèse* off Dieppe
8 Margaret Boggis, who had also been a Leading Stoker in the W.R.N.S.
9 The men from the Ostende lifeboat attaching a hawser to *Imp*'s stern
10 *Martha McGilda* by Deryk Foster
11 Entering a small harbour on the Normandy coast could present quite a challenge in an onshore gale
12 Noel Jordan, the first owner of *Martha McGilda*
13 *Martha* and author in the tiny harbour of Femø
14 My first sight of Finland, the sinister black lighthouse of Marhällan. *Photo:* Uno Markström
15 *Martha* at Simrisham, my favourite port in Sweden
16 *Martha* after her winter refit
17 *Martha* aground in Calais Harbour
18 A Dutch lifeboat in action off the Frisian Islands
19 Author collecting tickets from cars before they embarked on the *Free Enterprise* in Dover. *Photo: Evening Standard,* London

Illustrations

20 The crew of the *Free Enterprise* on the top deck. *Photo:* Ray Warner Ltd
21 Mother steering *Martha*
22 Captain J. E. Dawson, Master of M.V. *Free Enterprise*
23 *Roskilde* taking shape in McGruer's Yard
24 *Roskilde* takes to the sea for the first time—April 1974
25 *Roskilde* running before the wind
26 Peter Crago, John Munro and Victor Henry learning to sail *Martha* on the Thames
27 Captain Ian McLaren, our instructor at the School of Navigation
28 Texel out sailing in winter
29 Dick in mid-Channel
30 Waiting for his sea bird

ACKNOWLEDGEMENTS

I would like to thank the Editors of *Yachting Monthly* and the *R.N.S.A. Journal* for their kind permission to reprint some of the material which originally appeared in those magazines.

I would like to recall with gratitude and affection the previous owners of my first two boats; Mr Cutts and Noel Jordan, who did so much to inspire my earliest voyages; and to thank Mr Chippendale, the man who built some special magic into the Folkboat, *Martha McGilda*, thereby enabling me to sail so many thousands of happy miles.

I would also like to thank all my brave friends who risked their lives to accompany me on the *Imp* and *Martha McGilda*; especially Bunty, Winkle, Sue, Margaret, Daphne, Gillian and Barbara. And my many good friends around the coasts of Northern Europe who helped to make my annual voyages so wonderful.

Commodore Jack Dawson gave me invaluable help with chapters 10 and 11, and it is thanks to him and the splendid crew of *Free Enterprise I* that I enjoyed my life in the Merchant Navy so much.

Squadron Leader John Russell, who designed our beautiful cutter, *Roskilde*, and Mr James McGruer and all his fine craftsmen who built her, have been responsible for giving us many happy days at sea. And I would also like to give my special thanks to the boys from Forest Gate—Peter, Philip, John, David, Victor, Stephen, Mark and Jeff—who have helped so much to keep *Martha McGilda* afloat, and reminded me, by their expressions, of the half-forgotten wonder of learning to handle a boat for the complete novice.

And, finally, I would like to thank Rita Wadley who typed a large portion of the Ms, and made such an excellent job of decyphering the original, almost illegible, pages.

1. THE CALL OF THE SEA

Today is a day like any other—except for one miraculous difference. It is my BOAT day.

There are soft white clouds, like woolly sheep, ambling across the broad blue heavens above me; and out beyond the lock gates the whole river is on the move. The ebb tide is running fast, a seething torrent of grey-green liquid shot with darts of silver and gold. And all the big freighters and tugs towing coveys of lighters, the stately sailing-barges and squat pleasure-launches, the half-submerged logs and old plastic bottles are moving steadily eastwards, down towards the wide open sea.

'What perfect bliss!' I think to myself. 'But how sad for all those people who have never heard the call of the river, or the gentle song of the waves lapping against a clinker-built hull; or seen a slender mast which could reach right up to the stars in the sky . . .'.

Since early morning I have been kneeling on the foredeck scraping away at last year's salt-encrusted varnish, and pondering on how it all began.

* * * * *

We lived in a tall Victorian house in South Kensington when I was a child. It seemed a million miles away from the banks of the river, but whenever some plaintive little fog-horn called out in the night I would rush to the window in my long flannel nightdress and make desperate plans for running away to sea.

There was a girl who lived in our house, Jessie McNeil from the Outer Hebrides, who took me for walks in Hyde Park every Wednesday when my governess had her afternoon off. She resembled the heroine of some Viking saga with her flame-red hair, freckled face and far-away gaze, and she would talk to me for hours on end about the sea and ships. Her brother had been one of the crew on Scott's first expedition to the Antarctic, and she gave me a stone for my ninth birthday which he had actually picked up on Ross Island below Mount Erebus. I still have it to this day.

My father insisted that I should learn how to row at an early age, and he never refused me a shilling with which to hire a boat on the Serpentine after my morning's lessons were finished, despite my mother's anxious protests.

In those days my sea-going experiences consisted of an annual voyage to Gibraltar or Tangier aboard a P. & O. liner, and a cruise to West Africa in an old banana ship. Those were the best days of my childhood, and I lived from one April till the next with the throb of the great steam engines pounding in my ears, and the surge of the thundering Biscay combers mingling with the dancing sapphire waves of the Trade Wind belt. I never wanted to arrive anywhere—only to stay for ever and ever on those glorious ships, far away from the fetters of the land.

We left London when I was thirteen and went to live in Nottinghamshire, where I persuaded my parents to send me to the local grammar school. And it was there, in that ugly square building which I soon grew to love, that I first began to concentrate on geography, astronomy and maths, especially trigonometry; all subjects which I hoped would lead me to an understanding of navigation in the years to come.

I saved up my pocket-money for over a year to buy a prismatic compass, and with that bewitching toy I spent many happy hours in the school holidays taking bearings of distant objects and plotting my position on an Ordnance Survey map. I had one overwhelming ambition in life which never wavered or altered course; and that was to grow up as fast as possible so that I could join the W.R.N.S. and go to sea.

* * * * *

The Call of the Sea 3

A year or so later my dream came true. My father was wholeheartedly on my side and he arranged everything in a clandestine manner, so that when my calling-up papers suddenly arrived on the breakfast table one morning, it was already a *fait accompli*. My mother who, on her part, had done some secret manoeuvring to get me into the local Land Army so that she could keep an eye on me, felt that the whole affair was a dirty underhand plot. Nevertheless, I joined the W.R.N.S. when I was seventeen as a Stoker, 2nd Class, which was the only seagoing category in need of more recruits at that time.

'The lowest form of animal life in the whole perishing navy,' as we were described by the bo'sun at my first base, turned out to be the ideal life for me; and I spent two and a half years of perfect happiness looking after antiquated petrol and diesel engines on the liberty-boats in Portsmouth and Southampton.

I remember one particular winter's night when a southerly gale was blowing straight up Southampton Water, and the antiaircraft gun on the end of the Ocean Dock was firing at a lone German raider somewhere up among the constellation of Orion. There was quite a sea running with wind over tide, and solid foaming waves broke over the bows of our boat every few seconds. A rivulet of icy water funnelled off the rim of my tin helmet into a small persistent channel which found its way inside my oilskin collar and, eventually, down the back of my neck. All the sailors were singing *Danny Boy* as I leant over my noisy charge, an old 4-cylinder Kelvin engine, to make sure that the pistons were also singing their special rhythmic song despite the fury of the elements. And suddenly I knew, with a blinding flash of insight, that this was my ideal situation in life, something towards which I had felt a magnetic pull since my earliest childhood.

In due course I came home with the exalted rank of Leading Stoker, a W.R.N.S. Employment Certificate which said that I was a keen and conscientious member of the boat's crew who was suitable for re-engagement, and my love of the sea undiminished.

I had been inspired to study for a Yachtmaster's (Offshore) Certificate by my last coxswain in the W.R.N.S., a petty officer in her middle forties who had managed to pass the Board of

Trade examination and knew more about boats and the sea than anyone else I had ever met. I longed to follow in her footsteps, but soon discovered that this was impossible unless one had perfect eyesight without glasses. I was bitterly disappointed until some kind friend introduced me to a feasible compromise. Captain O. M. Watt's excellent correspondence course became the focus of my existence during that first year at home. I worked methodically through the twelve lessons, solved intricate problems about the mariner's compass, the rise and fall of the tides, fog pilotage and D.R.s and E.P.s; and ended up with a smart looking Coastal Navigation Certificate which convinced me that I knew just about everything to do with handling a boat in coastal waters—indeed, I might even teach the professional seamen a few new tricks!

* * * * *

I had two ex-Wren friends, Winkle and Sue, with whom I had kept in close touch after we were demobbed. Winkle, who had been the coxswain on our boat, was small and indomitable with brown curly hair and greenish eyes slanting upwards at the corners. She was very courageous and never minded how hard the wind blew or how many bombs dropped around us. Sue, who had been the deck-hand, was a tall blonde with blue eyes the size of ping-pong balls; the sort of girl who made an immediate and favourable impact on all men who came within her orbit. She was just finishing a course in cooking and floral decorations at the Cordon Bleu.

One glorious morning I summoned my two friends to an urgent meeting on the balcony of the Grapes, a small pub overlooking the river in Limehouse. Whenever we met, it always had to be somewhere near the river; somewhere with the music of ship's sirens and the lapping of waves against ancient wooden piles to remind us of the best years of our lives.

There was an atmosphere of volcanic excitement about that meeting, for we had come there to discuss an advertisement in *Yachting Monthly* which I had noticed the previous night. It ran as follows: 'Three ex-boat's crew Wrens required as deck-hands for 100 ton Bermudian-rigged cutter, leaving for Mediterranean on two year voyage early July.'

We could hardly believe our eyes as we gazed and gazed at those magic words. It was the sort of heaven-sent job we had so often dreamt about, but never seriously thought we should find it. The only fly in the ointment was the dread of telling our respective parents that we were proposing to go to sea for another two years.

By the time the first evening star had begun to twinkle above the top-mast of a schooner in the West India Docks, we had made up our minds and written a joint letter applying for the job.

An answer came by return of post inviting us to go for an interview aboard the S.Y. *Arabella*. The following day Sue and I travelled down to Southampton—Winkle had returned to her temporary job at some pony stables on Dartmoor by then—and we were met at the station by Mr Sedgwick Small, the owner of the yacht. He was a short, plump man with heavy jowls and a melon-shaped face above which his yachting cap was poised at a jaunty angle. He greeted us enthusiastically, bared a set of large yellowish teeth at Sue and invited us to join him for luncheon at the Polygon Hotel.

During the prawn cocktails Mr S.S., as we soon christened him, outlined his plans for the voyage to the Mediterranean. There would be himself, his wife and young daughter aboard, as well as a qualified skipper, a cook, two boys of sixteen and the three of us. Our wages would be £1 a week with all food provided, and we would share the work above and below-decks with the boys and the cook. He hoped to leave for Tangier at the end of July when his daughter's school holidays started; meanwhile we would go for a short trial cruise to Normandy and the Channel Islands.

After lunch Mr S.S. took us aboard *Arabella* at her anchorage off Hythe Pier. As we pulled towards her in the dinghy, the reflection from her sleek white hull came dancing across the calm grey river to meet us. She was an ex-19 metre racing yacht and had won the King's Cup in pre-war days. Built of teak on steel frames, she had an overall length of 95 feet and her slender mast, which rose to the spectacular height of 110 feet, could support more than 3,000 square feet of canvas. Her decks were as white and spotless as a polar landscape, and her brass fittings gleamed in the sunshine.

As soon as the owner was out of earshot Sue whispered to me: 'There must be an awful lot of work to do on this boat. I've never seen such a great shining monster before!'

Below-decks we received a striking impression of highly polished mahogany panelling, dainty chintz curtains drawn across the portholes to shield the cabins from prying eyes, and plenty of soft upholstery in the saloon. It was all very pretty, but somehow it struck a discordant note; I thought of the tough functional trimmings of our naval pinnaces, and wondered how we should get on out at sea.

The only other crew member aboard that day was Dolly, the cook. A small dispirited-looking woman with wispy beige-coloured hair and sharp features, she surveyed us briefly without enthusiasm, then retired into her own rather smelly quarters.

Mr S.S. asked us a number of searching questions about our backgrounds, pastimes and morals, but nothing about our nautical expertise, which surprised me. During a pause in the conversation I suddenly displayed my Coastal Navigation Certificate, feeling sure that it would make a deep impression on him and, perhaps, clinch the matter of our employment: but my pride suffered a severe blow when he merely pushed it aside with a fat pink hand which resembled a neurotic piglet, and growled something about wishing to engage a common-or-garden deck-hand and NOT another skipper!

Despite that momentary unpleasantness, he offered us the jobs—perhaps he'd had no other applicants—and agreed to take Winkle on spec, as we made it quite clear that we would not sail without her.

Arabella was due to leave England in ten days' time, and Mr S.S. asked us to join her at Hamble on June 26th at the latest.

* * * * *

On the morning of the Great Day Sue travelled down to Hamble from her home near Winchester, while Winkle and I caught a train from Waterloo. A shrill whistle blew and we hung out of the windows waving frantically to our small group of parents with their crumpled handkerchiefs, until they faded away into the smoke haze behind us. It was a moment of supreme misery and we hardly spoke a word all the way to Southampton.

An hour or so later we reached Hamble Jetty and found Tony, one of the new cadets, waiting for us in the dinghy. The son of a local policeman, he was a tall gangling boy with his hair close-cropped, apart from a ragged tuft jutting out over his friendly smiling face.

'I bet the old man won't half create when he sees all that gear!' he surmised with a giggle, as he hoisted my guitar-case into the bows on top of a pair of large suit-cases, a kit-bag full of books, a duffel-coat and some sea-boots.

I surveyed my luggage with some misgivings. It had seemed a modest enough pile in London, but suddenly it appeared to have grown out of all proportion, especially when one compared it with Winkle's neat little hold-all into which she had managed to cram all her belongings. I had hated the thought of leaving my guitar behind for two years; then there were those heavy books—Nicholls's *Seamanship and Nautical Knowledge* (from which I had never been parted since my eighteenth birthday), Nansen's *Farthest North*, John Masefield's *Collected Poems*—not to mention a number of other indispensable treasures.

Tony was right. Mr Sedgwick Small *did* create; but not nearly as much as he created the following day after my parents had paid a surprise visit to the yacht, shortly before we were due to sail.

'I bet you won't last for long, my girl!' grinned Andy, the other cadet. 'You should have taken a decko at the old man's face when he handed your mater over the side!'

'Don't be so horrid,' I replied. 'It won't make the slightest difference once we get away to sea.'

'I hope you're right,' murmured the skipper who had just joined our group in the fo'c'sle. Alan Ramsay was an ex-R.A.F. Mosquito pilot with a strong rugged face and humorous lines around his grey eyes. He looked the sort of man who would not tolerate fools or hypocrites.

The arrival of Mrs Sedgwick Small caused a diversion which brought us all up on deck. As the dinghy approached we could see a well-upholstered lady wearing tight linen slacks and an Aertex blouse which fitted her like a grape-skin, eyeing the

Arabella with a certain veiled hostility. Her thick copper-red hair was arranged in tight curls around her pale full-moon face, and her scarlet finger-nails beat a steady tattoo on the stern thwart of the dinghy. Suddenly she swivelled right round to fix Sue with a disparaging stare. A minute later we retired tactfully below, as it was clear that Mr S.S. was experiencing some difficulty in getting his spouse to negotiate the guard-rail without splitting her trousers.

After tea we set sail for France. Even before the anchor was stowed and the dinghy lashed down there was a distinct air of tension on deck; an uncertainty as to who was in command. The skipper paced to and fro on the after deck while his employer spun the wheel in a showy manner, shouted contradictory orders at his bewildered crew and wove a perilous passage through the crowded anchorage with the throttles of both engines advanced to full ahead.

Winkle and I had spent several hours washing up piles of dirty dishes and peeling potatoes in the dark steaming-hot galley, with Dolly constantly chivvying us and making sarcastic remarks about our lack of speed and know-how; so it was a great relief to emerge on deck and help with the work of getting under way. But no sooner had *Arabella* settled on to her course towards the Nab Tower, than Mr S.S. ordered us below again to prepare the supper. His wife and Dolly had disappeared into their cabins before the anchor chain was hove short.

An hour or so later the yacht swung round on to her course for Le Havre. There was no wind so the engines were kept running at full speed ahead. Presently our long vibrating hull met the Channel swell for the first time and, simultaneously, I began to feel very seasick. There was a loin of salt pork suspended from the deck-head in the fo'c'sle, over the table where we ate our meals, and it had begun to describe a series of arcs just above our heads at the same time emitting a powerful meaty odour which was hard to ignore. All my romantic notions about running away to sea were swiftly replaced by an urgent desire to scramble up on deck and reach the ship's side before it was too late!

At midnight Mr S.S. took the wheel and Alan sent us to bed. But less than four hours later our employer personally woke us and told us to get a move on and start holystoning the decks for two or three hours, until it was time to cook the breakfast. The swell had increased and we all felt tired, hungry and sick.

A fresh breeze arose with the sun, so we hoisted the huge mainsail with the owner shouting abuse at us while that great thrashing monster threatened to whisk us overboard. It was a back-breaking task, and once it was set Alan took him aside to explain that we had never been to sea in a sailing-ship before and must be given a chance to learn. He was brusquely told to mind his own business.

Mrs S.S. and Dolly had been seasick in their cabins for most of the night, and our next job was to take them some light refreshments and clear up the mess. Everyone seemed relieved when *Arabella* finally dropped anchor in the outer harbour in Le Havre. Mrs S.S. put a tousled head through the for'ard hatch and called her husband an insensitive pig for abandoning her to her fate during that hellish crossing.

'*Pas devant leckypage!*' he growled at her in his execrable French, imagining that we were too ignorant to understand.

It took us one whole hour to furl the sails, coil the ropes and wash the salt water off the varnished hatch-covers. By that time we were so tired that we could hardly crawl below and into our bunks.

* * * * *

While *Arabella* was crossing the Channel to Normandy, my father had not been idle at home. By some devious means he had unearthed a number of sordid details about the Sedgwick Smalls of which we were blissfully ignorant. It appeared that Mr S.S. was an undischarged bankrupt who was anxious to wind up his affairs and leave England as soon as possible. His name had figured in a very unsavoury legal case which had caused quite a stir at the time. His wife, who was thought to be the owner of the yacht, was a woman of means who had previously owned a hotel and an amusement arcade at a well known seaside resort. Their plans for the future were shrouded in mystery, but seemed unlikely to be of a respectable nature . . .

Thoroughly alarmed by this report, my father wrote to his old friend, Sir Alexander Coutanche, the Bailiff of Jersey, asking him to intercept the yacht and try to persuade me to return home immediately.

* * * * *

We spent three days in Le Havre; long hard days of slave labour. Up at four each morning for the daily ritual of holystoning the decks, then several hours of disagreeable chores below-decks which included cleaning out the galley, heads and the Sedgwick Small's state-room, as they pompously referred to their luxurious cabin. Later the boys rowed us ashore in the dinghy and we spent the rest of the day filling the heavy water-casks, and cleaning brass fittings which had turned green with many years of neglect. We used to sit on the beach near the water's edge and scour them with wet sand, then rub and rub and rub ... Although it was hard work, we got on well with Alan and the boys and enjoyed ourselves enormously away from the nagging tongues and prying eyes aboard the yacht.

In the evenings we wandered around the war-ravaged city, and often made a glass of *vin ordinaire* last for an hour or more in some dockside café. We were always tired and hungry, but £1 a week would not run to meals ashore.

I had not yet dared to play my guitar, and it stood in its case in a corner of our cabin regarding me reproachfully. I often suspected Dolly of tampering with it while we were ashore, and one day I left a rude message just inside the lid; the result confirmed my suspicions, as I found an extra large pile of dirty dishes left for me to wash up that evening!

'People like you lot don't know the meaning of hard work,' was the prelude to her favourite dirge when we returned from four hours' hard labour on the beach. 'Take me, for example. I started work in the cotton mills when I was fourteen, and I never had no time to go gallivanting round pubs and cafés and suchlike ...' (taking an exploratory sniff at Sue who was standing nearest to her).

'Come off it, Dolly!' groaned the skipper. 'If you weren't such an old drip someone might ask you out one day.'

On July 1st we set sail for Cherbourg. It was a boisterous olive-green day with great white horses galloping into the Seine

The Call of the Sea

estuary. We sped past a dredger outside the harbour entrance, and a man on her bridge shouted '*Bon voyage, mes cocottes!*' as he raised a bottle of wine to his lips.

Mr S.S. had ordered all 3,000 square feet of canvas to be set that morning, and *Arabella* flew across the shining seas with her lee rail awash and her whole hull throbbing with a wonderful *joie de vivre*, like some mighty sea-bird from the Southern Ocean spreading its wings for flight. We all agreed that it was worth putting up with any amount of beastliness to spend a day like that at sea.

A fierce argument soon broke out between Mr S.S. and the skipper, who had laid off a direct course from Le Havre to the Pointe de Barfleur.

'Take her down into the Seine Bay,' snapped the owner. 'If the wind freshens up my wife may wish to make for the nearest harbour.'

Alan pointed out that we should be on a lee shore, and *Arabella* drew too much water to enter most of the harbours anyway; also there were some outlying shoals along the Calvados coast.

Mr S.S.'s eyes began to bulge like a strangulated frog, and he grabbed the steering-wheel from Andy and swung it round 40° to port. The skipper stood near the mast with his chin jutting out like a granite ledge, and his eyes glittering with a cold grey light. Suddenly it dawned on me that our employer was a conceited old idiot who knew next to nothing about navigation, and was quite capable of wrecking *Arabella* in one of his tantrums.

Perhaps sensing the trend of my thoughts, he sent me below to prepare some sandwiches for lunch. The loin of pork was cleaving the air of the fo'c'sle in a most extraordinary way, and Mrs S.S. had managed to be sick all over the thick pile carpet in her state-room.

Alan, noticing the greenish colour of my face when I eventually emerged with the food, told Mr S.S. that he needed all the deck-hands on deck in future; and, anyway, why couldn't Dolly prepare the lunch if she had been engaged as our cook? The owner began to snarl unpleasantly, but suddenly his attention was arrested by the sight of huge breakers crashing on to the rocky ledges of Les Essarts de Langrune right ahead. At the same moment the skipper had ordered the yacht to be put about on the port tack, and he stood on guard behind the wheel wearing his defy-me-if-you-dare expression. Mr S.S., grasping his defeat, retired grumpily below where he remained for the next few hours. Later that evening he announced magnanimously that the three girls might have the honour of staying on deck all night, as the boys were too young for night watches.

Despite the skipper's intervention Winkle and I had spent a miserable few hours in the galley, and it was already dark when we struggled out on deck. The full moon hung, like some gigantic Chinese lantern, above the eastern horizon and there were a million stars twinkling in the dark blue heavens above us. Out to sea a dozen or more fishing-boats bowed and curtsied to the stars, acknowledging their superior brilliance in the universal scheme of things.

I took the helm at midnight, and we sailed along the path of the moon with a bow wave of glittering emeralds, where our stem threw asunder the phosphorescent sea. *Arabella* was no longer just a large expensive yacht, but a marvellous vibrant creature of straining wood and canvas singing a hauntingly beautiful song as she flew across the night seas.

Sue, Winkle and the skipper wedged themselves on the sloping deck beside me, and we felt quite drunk with the glory of our surroundings. Alan pointed out some of the brightest stars in the summer sky—Capella, Arcturus, Vega, Altair and Antares—and showed us how to find them on his star chart. Then we all recited our favourite sea poems, and the immortal lines of John Masefield and Rudyard Kipling drifted away into the silvery moonlight.

At eight o'clock next morning we dropped anchor in the Petite Rade at Cherbourg. Mr S.S. had re-appeared on deck ten minutes beforehand, looking fresh and rested after a long night's sleep. He took the helm from Winkle and gave us a lecture on our appearance when entering harbour. It was not well received considering we had been on deck all night.

* * * * *

Our days in Cherbourg were similar to those in Le Havre, only worse. We were much more tired and hungry by then, and the holiday-makers on the beach eyed us rather strangely, wondering perhaps if we were a gang of convicts doing some type of forced labour.

Although we saw very little of Mrs S.S., she made her presence felt all the time; she and Dolly were heartily disliked by all the crew.

At dawn on the fourth morning I glanced at the barometer and noticed that it had fallen dramatically. A French yachtsman who was rowing past us in his dinghy predicted that it would soon be the sort of weather in which you would not even put your mother-in-law outside! Mr S.S. sniffed contemptuously and ordered the full range of canvas to be hoisted immediately.

The voyage round Cap de la Hague and through the Alderney Race in a rising gale and confused breaking seas was quite hair-raising, and the yacht was inclined at such a fearful angle that it caused havoc down below and great anxiety to our skipper.

'The man's a raving lunatic,' he muttered, when our employer was out of earshot. 'Her mast's far too tall and she's shipping too much water for this kind of caper. And he knew damn well we shouldn't have enough sea-room to reef among all these rocks.'

Despite his gloomy soliloquy the skipper brought us safely into harbour at St Peter Port. There was a large crowd assembled on the jetty to watch *Arabella*'s arrival, so Mr S.S. pushed Alan aside and, grabbing the wheel himself, he steered towards the inner harbour.

Presently a violent gust of wind caught our stern and, swinging it right round, smashed the rudder against a groin which was jutting out from the Castle Pier.

'Fend her off can't you, you hopeless bunch of cretins!' roared the helmsman, his face contorted into an ugly red pumpkin.

A few minutes later we reached the drying out slip and moored the yacht in total silence. Then Alan took us ashore to eat fish and chips and visit his favourite pubs. Just before closing time he confided to me that *Arabella* was not at all the kind of set-up he had been led to understand, and he would be damned if he spent the next two years toadying round after Mr S.S.

* * * * *

Arabella was up on the slip for several days, and we spent many hours scrubbing her enormous slimy bottom with long-handled brooms. On the second morning the mail caught up with us, and Mr S.S. must have received some disquieting information about my father's investigations into his background. I knew nothing about this at the time, but soon became aware of a virulent hostility directed specifically at me.

We left Guernsey on a gentle blue and gold morning, with deep violet shadows here and there where the jagged rocks arose sharp and menacing out of the strong swirling tides. *Arabella* ran goose-winged before the northerly breeze, with Mr S.S. at the helm and his crew splicing ropes up for'ard.

A few hours later the coast of Jersey was under our lee, the mainsail furled and engines running, and everything shipshape for entering harbour. The yacht advanced steadily towards the Albert Pier in St Helier and, simultaneously, a black Rolls-Royce, flying a pennant from the end of its bonnet, advanced inexorably towards the same place. Mr S.S. trained his telescope on to that formidable limousine while I hid behind the mast, for already I had recognized the distinguished profile of my father's old friend, Sir Alexander Coutanche. The mooring lines were hardly secured before the Bailiff of Jersey had lowered himself on to the deck, shaken hands with Mr S.S. and asked that I should be released that evening to dine with him and his family at St Aubin.

The Sedgwick Smalls invited him to come below and have a glass of sherry, and they were both fairly bubbling with charm and amiability. While Sue and I served the drinks and savoury titbits, Mrs S.S. smiled at me in affectionate motherly fashion and told me to run along and get changed, at the same time giving me a playful pat on the rear quarters. I was so astonished that I nearly dropped the sherry decanter.

Back in the fo'c'sle Tony threw me a sympathetic glance: 'Bet you five quid your days are numbered, my love. Expect they'll give you the chop as soon as we clear this island. Cheer up old thing! [Seeing that I was about to dissolve into tears;] It's a dog's life in this floating coffin and you can't be any worse off at home!'

I spent a very pleasant evening with the Coutanches, and

they were intelligent enough not to try and persuade me to leave *Arabella*. They just told me about my father's findings and left it at that.

The following evening I sealed my own fate by accidentally throwing the lid of Mrs S.S.'s silver teapot overboard while I was doing the washing-up. It lay concealed in the murky depths of the bowl after I had finished a big pile of cups and saucers; and when I threw the dirty water over the side a fleeting glint of silver caught my eye, as the lid flashed by on its last journey to the bottom of the harbour. Not surprisingly, Mrs S.S. was furious when she heard what I had done. She accused me of wilful negligence, gross incompetence, despicable laziness and various other undesirable tendencies which had no direct link with the teapot disaster.

We left Jersey that evening and, as usual, the crew only had three or four hour's sleep before it was time to crawl on deck and start holystoning those vile strips of teak. I was not feeling at my best when Mr S.S. sent for me after breakfast. He cleared his throat noisily once or twice and invited me to sit down, which I interpreted as an ominous sign. Gazing fixedly at some interesting object on the bulkhead to the left of my face, he began by telling me how upset his wife had been about her silver teapot lid but, quite apart from that unfortunate incident, she had found my work below-decks far from satisfactory.

'And, furthermore,' he continued pompously, clearly about to strike a richer seam. 'I have no intention of harbouring a deck-hand aboard my yacht whose friends and relatives feel free to drop in on me whenever the inclination takes them—Do I make myself quite clear?'

Before I could put up any sort of defence, he had given me the sack.

We had a calm grey voyage back to England, but for me it passed in a blurred haze of misery. I had gone to sea with my two certificates and a puffed up opinion of my own value aboard a boat; and here was I three weeks later, the only one to get the sack. And it wasn't as if I hadn't tried . . .

I reached Waterloo early one evening, and took a taxi back home (we had returned to London soon after I left the W.R.N.S.). As it turned the corner into our street, I saw my father standing outside the house looking anxiously to the right and left. He had no idea what time I was due to arrive, and it occurred to me that he might have been standing there for a very long time. And suddenly I knew that I was glad to be home again.

* * * * *

The *Arabella* saga, as far as we were concerned, only lasted for another three months. The skipper left a few days after me, and several others followed him in quick succession before the yacht reached Tangier. Some curious cargo was stowed in the bilges about that time, and as soon as she reached her next port of call, Marseilles, Winkle and Sue were given the sack without any apparent reason. As they had spent most of their meagre wages on extra food and Mr S.S. refused to pay their fares back home, they were stranded in France in a semi-starving condition and had to seek assistance from the British Consul.

The last we heard of *Arabella* was a terse paragraph in the *Daily Telegraph* to say that she had been fired on by Italian gunboats off Genoa, and was then escorted into harbour and confiscated from her owners. We never heard of them again.

2. A BOAT OF MY OWN

I knelt on the floor outside the library door with one ear glued to the keyhole and the other one pricked up, like a rabbit downwind of a weasel, to forestall the first hint of approaching footsteps on the stairs. I had no wish to be caught in that compromising position, but the *tête-à-tête* going on inside the library was far too crucial to be missed. My mother was doing most of the talking while my father sat peacefully in his big arm-chair, attempting to read *The Times*—

'You know the plumber who's fixing the kitchen boiler?' she addressed the back of his head. 'Well he came to work this morning looking very sunburnt and cheerful, and said he'd just had the best week-end of his life on some little boat off the Essex coast. Apparently his friend, who owns this boat, wants to sell it as he's building a larger one . . .'

A non-committal grunt came from the depths of the armchair.

'If the child had a boat of her own,' my mother suggested tentatively, 'it might perhaps settle her and stop her going off on all those very undesirable voyages in other people's boats?'

'Good idea!' approved the overseas news page, endorsing its assent with a sharp crackle. Uncontrollable shivers of excitement caused me to lose my balance at that moment, and I fell flat on my face on the hall floor.

Ten minutes later a telegram was dispatched to a Mr Cutts at West Mersea—'Wish to view your boat tomorrow. Please do not sell before. Manvers.'

We travelled to West Mersea early next morning, and I shall never forget the unique and indescribable thrill of standing on the Essex mud-flats gazing across the still grey water at that funny little boat, so like my childhood pictures of Noah's Ark. She nodded to me in the wash of a passing coaster and seemed to whisper; 'I'm just the sort of boat you're looking for!'

Needless to say we were putty in Mr Cutts' rough capable hands, as neither my mother nor I knew the first thing about buying a boat. But he was a nice man who loved his old boat dearly—indeed, he was most reluctant to part with her when he grasped that we had come to talk business and not just to sniff around.

The *Imp*, as she was called, had been a life-boat on a brand new collier, the S.S. *Ament*, which sailed out of Sunderland in 1930 and broke her back on the Long Sand on her maiden voyage. Although the mother ship was a total wreck, her lifeboats were salvaged and towed into Harwich to be sold by auction. The *Imp* was converted into a cabin-cruiser, propelled by a 16 h.p. petrol engine taken from a 1920 Humber car. Clinker built, with larch planking on a good solid backbone of English oak, her length was 24 feet 6 inches, her beam 7 feet 8 inches, and her draught just under 3 feet. She had a small mast stepped in a tabernacle on the cabin-top, and a loose-footed mainsail of miniature proportions. There was a large open cockpit dominated by the engine casing, and a comparatively spacious cabin with a bunk on either side, a raised skylight under which there was standing headroom, a small cooking area at the foot of the port bunk and three hooks on which to hang one's surplus clothing.

'Where is the lavatory?' enquired my mother, who likes to establish the more commonplace details early on.

'All you need is a good strong bucket in a boat o' this size,' replied Mr Cutts with a touch of severity. 'Them Baby Blakes an' suchlike is a snare an' a dissolution to the unsuspectin' seafarer—all them little pipes an' drain'oles in the bottom of a boat, jus' askin' for the sea to come rushin' in! D'you follow me?'

A Boat of My Own

My mother looked doubtful; but neither of us wished to give the impression that we did not follow him, so we nodded our heads sagely.

Mr Cutts was asking £250 for the *Imp*—once he had stopped muttering about having the ground swept away from under his feet and could be persuaded to ask anything. I had £100 which my grandmother had left me in War Savings Bonds, and my parents had promised to make up the difference. A neighbour who knew about buying boats insisted that we must get her surveyed: so a man from Tough's at Teddington went down to look at her a few days later and reported quite favourably, apart from one small item—'It was noticed that no electrical starting was fitted, and we think it would be rather a handful for a young lady to start this engine.'

I assured everyone who showed signs of interfering that this was no problem, as I had been starting marine engines by hand for three years without the slightest difficulty.

And suddenly the great day arrived when the *Imp* became MY VERY OWN BOAT.

* * * * *

I had invited a distant Italian cousin, Bunty Delmonte, to accompany me on the *Imp*'s maiden voyage. She and I had been out mackerel fishing together off the Brittany coast on one occasion—her family spent every summer in Dinard—and I had formed the impression, although I did not know her at all well, that she was an outdoor girl who adored the sea and small boats.

Bunty and I set off from West Mersea on a cool August morning, bound for the River Thames. There was a fresh easterly wind blowing in from the North Sea, and the *Imp* plunged defiantly into the green breaking seas which rushed to meet us as soon as we had rounded the south-west corner of Mersea Island.

My ears were still tingling with Mr Cutts' final words of advice. He had insisted on starting the engine himself, and he kept up his fussy monologue about weather forecasts, sandbanks, spring tides and wet sparking-plugs until we had cast off the moorings and finally escaped out of earshot.

Certainly the Blackwater estuary seemed a bit rougher than I had led my trusting cousin to expect, and the broad open cockpit seemed less advantageous than it had done on the day when my mother and I first viewed the boat, now that we were getting soaked by the stinging salt spray which was exploding over our heads every few seconds and making it very hard to see where one was going.

I remembered to turn right at the N.W. Knoll Buoy, and steadying my miniature compass on to a course of 205° magnetic, I steered towards the breaking seas on the Buxey Sand. The East Coast was quite unlike anything I had been used to; all those dismal bits of wood—'beacons' Mr Cutts had called them—sticking up out of the sea; birds actually STANDING not far from the boat (what on earth were they standing on?). And that tremendously strong salty smell, with miles and miles of brownish-green water covered with vicious white-crested waves.

Bunty crouched uncomfortably between the cabin bulkhead and the engine, and I noticed a pair of startled brown eyes peering at me from under a red pirate's cap, for she had just caught sight of the seething cauldron of white water towards which we were heading. 'What do you know about navigation?' she demanded anxiously.

I remembered a paragraph from Captain Watts' coastal navigation course which I quoted for her benefit: 'Navigation was never learned in a day. Put what you have learned into practice and don't be afraid to make mistakes. People who never make mistakes, never make anything.'

This proved to be an unhappy choice and did little to reassure her. Nevertheless, we navigated safely through the Ray Sand Channel and emerged into the River Crouch about the same time as the engine, which had been coughing and spluttering ominously for some while, finally petered out.

'Well, at least we can enjoy a few minutes peace!' I giggled brightly, attempting to be flippant for Bunty's sake. 'I'll just have a squint at the engine and see what's gone wrong.'

Of course I had no idea what had caused the engine to stop, and it soon became transparently clear that nothing I could do would induce it to start again. Bunty looked cold and frightened, and muttered something about wishing she'd never left home.

A Boat of My Own

Feeling very guilty about having invited her to come with me, I crawled precariously on to the heaving cabin-top and hoisted the tiny red canvas sail. 'I'll show her that I'm still in charge of our fate!' I thought to myself without much conviction.

But what with the wind blowing hard and steadily from the north-east and the spring ebb rushing out to sea, it was not long before our brave little boat had run aground and settled firmly on to the Maplin Sands, a few hundred yards from the bleak north-east corner of Foulness Island.

Altogether we spent twenty-two hours on that desolate sandbank. I placed our one and only fisherman's anchor as far out as the frail rusty chain would allow, then tried to light the stove to make some hot soup; but this proved impossible because of the angle at which we had dried out. We warmed ourselves by pumping out the very full bilges instead, then ate some rather stale sandwiches and settled down in the sloping cockpit to wait for the turn of the tide.

Towards nightfall we reviewed our miserable situation with growing despair. It was much colder by then, and the freezing wind sliced through our thin jerseys and slacks, causing our teeth to chatter continually. Presently the sea came rushing in and the *Imp* began to pound on the sands: at last she came afloat and swung wildly round her anchor, with nothing but the rusty old chain between our present exposed position and possible disaster. The engine was quite dead, and even when I did succeed in turning the hefty starting-handle, not a cough or a murmur escaped from that ancient relic.

Bunty, who had grown up in Naples under the German occupation, began to relive the horrors of her childhood as our plight became more hopeless. I felt very sorry for her, and also exceedingly hungry, cold and frightened myself. I had no idea if the anchor was dragging or not, as there were no lights on that dismal corner of Foulness Island with which to fix one's position. Out to sea the Mid Barrow Lightvessel and the Shivering Sand Tower added their powerful flashes to the necklace of glittering buoys around the sandbanks, but I was too numbed with cold and anxiety to take bearings and try to determine our exact position.

When I had first joined the W.R.N.S., old Chiefie, our

instructor at the Mechanical Training Establishment in Portsmouth, often used to say: 'Don't think of your engine as a cold bit of metal, girls, but as a 'uman being what's got to be fed and watered and cared for, same as you and me!'

His words came back to me out on the Maplin Sands, and I remember making two important vows that night. First, that I would spare no efforts to learn everything possible about my engine at the earliest opportunity: and secondly, that I would never take anyone to sea again who did not know exactly what they were in for.

Around five o'clock the first grey light of dawn revealed the wet sands emerging from the cold black sea once more, and the Whitaker Beacon outlined against the eastern sky like some Viking sentinel guarding the East Anglian approaches.

'For God's sake let's wade ashore,' implored Bunty, who had stopped burbling about the Gestapo by then.

I felt sad and depressed at having to leave the *Imp* all alone, but it seemed the most sensible thing to do. As we stumbled through the glutinous black mud on to the Essex saltings, a policeman rose up from behind a windswept tussock and ordered us to follow him. We were bundled into the back of a rural Black Maria and driven swiftly inland to the Foulness police station.

'Poor little *Imp*!' I thought tragically, as I caught one final glimpse of the North Sea through the barred rear window of the van.

Twenty minutes later Bunty and I were devouring fried eggs and bacon and drinking large mugs of tea in our captor's home, while he explained to us that the island was a military zone on which no one was allowed to land without a special permit: and our boat was situated right in the middle of an artillery practice range. However, seeing that we came under the heading of shipwrecked mariners, he would do his best to help us.

Later that morning our kind policeman brought a mechanic across the sands to visit the *Imp*. He peered inside the engine casing for two minutes, then straightened up and looked at me pityingly: 'Not much wrong with 'er, I reckon. All that water in the bilges, spraying on to the magneto orff of your flywheel. That's what's gorn an' done it, I reckon. Always keep your mag an' your plugs dry, young woman, an' you won't come to no 'arm.'

The tide was flooding fast. As soon as the *Imp* began to float he tinkered briefly inside the engine cover then gave a brisk pull at the starting-handle and, lo and behold, the engine roared into life. Just when everything was beginning to assume a rosy aspect, Bunty announced that she wished to go straight back to London and NOT by sea. I couldn't really blame her, the way things had turned out. So we motored into the River Crouch and down the Roach to Havengore Creek, where we left the *Imp* on a mooring and said goodbye to our friends, the policeman and the mechanic.

'Mind how you go,' they called after us, as we boarded the bus for Shoeburyness. 'You'll always be welcome on the Maplins any time you're passing this way!'

Two weeks later I returned to Havengore to fetch the *Imp* with a friend who had been at sea for two years, and we had no problems in bringing her up the Thames on a fine Sunday.

By that time I was a member of the Hurlingham Yacht Club which had moorings on the river at Putney, and I spent the next year or so getting to know my boat and going for cruises in company to the estuaries of the Thames and Medway. Many of the members had built their own boats, and they were a cheerful friendly crowd who looked after each other well, and never minded giving a tow to someone whose engine was proving temperamental or who had inadvertently run aground. I bought a smart yachting cap with the club's gold badge on the front, and I made a point of waving to the captains of all the biggest ships I passed on the river—one captain waving to another, as I told myself.

Winkle or Sue often accompanied me on those week-end voyages, and on fine summer nights when the sea was glowing with phosphorescence we would spend hours stirring up the water to see the sparkling emeralds darting around the hull of the boat. Sometimes I would fill an empty milk bottle with that magic liquid in the hopes of keeping it alive all through the week. But it was like the wind or the sunshine, that glorious phosphorescence ... there are some things you can never conserve in a bottle.

My mother's intuition had certainly proved to be correct, as the ownership of the *Imp* was having a stabilizing effect on me. I was intensely proud of her and felt convinced that she was the most perfect and desirable vessel that had ever been launched. The fact that she leaked like a sieve and required several thousand strokes on a prehistoric pump every day to keep the water level below the deck-boards, mattered not at all. Also I had grown accustomed to sharing my sleeping-bag with the magneto on damp cold nights, to make sure that it was dry enough to ignite the engine next morning.

During the second year of the *Imp* I decided to make a bold dash to Amsterdam and back during my two weeks' summer holiday. Winkle had agreed to take part in this daring enterprise, and we set off down the Thames in high spirits at the end of July.

After riding out a gale at anchor near the mouth of the River Swale, we rounded the North Foreland two days later and had our first taste of the open sea. The weather was fine and sunny and the *Imp* responded happily to the confused swell, where the English Channel meets the North Sea for the first time. The muscles in our arms had become hard and strong from our daily spells at the pump, and by the time we reached Dover Winkle and I felt ready to conquer the Seven Seas.

We laid in a good stock of provisions, and I was given an impressive document by the Dover customs which announced that 'the Ship, *Imp*, under her Master, R. Pierrepont, was bound for the Port of Calais and other places beyond the seas with two persons on board.'

It was a grey windy day when the *Imp* finally put to sea on her first Channel crossing. We had taken the precaution of buying a bottle of rum before leaving Dover, but I noticed with some anxiety that there was a muffled booming noise issuing from its neck as soon as we pulled the cork to drink a toast to our departure. This had a discouraging effect on me, coupled with the sinister coughing and spluttering noises made by the engine; also the bilge water was rushing to and fro beneath the deck-boards and our small world had begun to heave up and down in a most alarming manner.

Our navigational instruments consisted of my small prismatic compass, which I had bought when I was fourteen, a pair of Captain Field's Improved parallel rules, a chart of the Dover Strait, a motorist's map of Belgium and Holland and a book called *The English Channel Handbook*, published by the Hydrographic Department of the Admiralty in 1943, intended for the use of commando units who were planning raids on the French coast.

We took turns of an hour each at the helm and it was during the second hour, when England had disappeared from sight and we were feeling rather lonely and pessimistic, that the *Thing* happened . . .

Winkle was steering while I pumped out the bilges, when she casually mentioned that it was becoming more and more difficult to keep the *Imp* on course. I had complete confidence in her ability to handle a boat under the most trying conditions, so I replied 'what a nuisance!' or something equally fatuous, and continued pulling the pump handle up and down.

Some while later we noticed that there were more whitecrested waves around us, which continually burst over the cabin-top in clouds of ice-cold spray. Winkle asked me to steer while she hung over the stern to examine the rudder. Suddenly she shouted, 'the blade's not there any more!'

I hauled her back into the cockpit by her feet, engaged the clutch in neutral, and then we sat down on the engine casing to review our dismal situation. It appeared that the blade of the rudder had snapped right across, leaving nothing but a thin jagged edge with which it was impossible for the helmsman to control the direction of the boat. We were at least twelve miles from England, and goodness knows how many more from France as we were by no means certain of our exact position; and the wind, which was already a good Force 5, was freshening all the time. To face the bare facts, we were sitting in a leaky old boat out in the middle of the Dover Strait, unable to move in any given direction, and there was not another ship in sight.

At that stage I realized with crystal clarity that I was not cut out to be the heroine of some great maritime drama—a sort of Grace Darling of the English Channel: indeed, I found it hard enough to summon up a single coherent thought with which to tackle our unfortunate predicament. Luckily Winkle behaved with her usual quiet courage and, managing to keep a cheerful expression on her face, she opened the rum bottle and poured us out two stiff toddies. Once well fortified, we set to work to concoct our brain-wave.

Inspired by the sight of the bread knife rolling about on the cabin floor, I seized a section of the engine casing with trembling hands and sawed out a rectangular panel of wood: then I hung over the stern, with Winkle gripping my ankles, and after what seemed a very long time I succeeded in marrying the new piece of wood to the jagged remnants of the rudder with my best suspender belt, held rigidly in position by some strong codline lashings. Winkle gently pushed the tiller from one side to the other with the engine going slow ahead, and I could see that my masterpiece was beginning to exert a minimal pull on the water astern. The next moment I hung over the side and was violently seasick.

We plotted a reverse bearing on our chart, making unusually big allowances for tide and leeway, then set off across the rolling beam seas towards the English coast. One or other of us pumped continually to make sure that our vital magneto, which had spent a warm night in my sleeping-bag, remained comparatively dry and responsive. About three hours later, much to our intense relief and astonishment, the *Imp* motored crabwise through the eastern entrance of Dover Harbour and on through the narrow gully leading into the Camber Dock. We moored alongside a tug called the S.T. *Rumania* in a secluded corner of the dock, and Winkle went into the cabin to make a pot of tea.

After a while the triumph and excitement of our safe return to Dover began to wear off, and I felt waves of sadness sweeping over me. I sat on the stern gazing despondently at our makeshift rudder and listening to the plaintive crying of the gulls high up on the cliff-face above the Camber. Presently a strongly-built man with ginger hair, wearing a rather striking Fair Isle pullover, leant over the bulwarks of the tug and asked me what the matter was. I told him about our attempt to cross to France and our misfortunes in mid-Channel: I may have looked as if I was likely to burst into tears, for he suddenly swung round and bawled down the open hatch for Haggis to come on deck. He then introduced himself as Captain Griffiths, the skipper of the tug; and I felt convinced that the spirit of chivalry flourished in the good old-fashioned way behind that gruff unsmiling façade.

By the time Winkle reappeared with the teapot, the remains of our rudder lay on the after deck of the tug and the skipper was on his hands and knees taking measurements and barking crisp instructions at Haggis, a seaman of Scottish extraction, about getting the special piece of wood that he would require.

Suddenly I began to feel quite cheerful for we had obviously fallen into good hands and would soon be able to put to sea again. We poured out mugs of strong tea for the crew of the *Rumania*, as well as ourselves and a petty officer from a neighbouring torpedo-boat who had come across to join the party. He was newly married and very pleased with himself, and he seemed to think that I needed some fatherly advice . . .

'You don't want to waste too much of your time messing about in boats, my girl,' he counselled. 'I've seen one or two females quite besotted with them in my time. Your best place is in the home learning how to cook and bring up children, and if I was you I'd get rid of that old tub and concentrate on getting a man instead!'

I did not care for his remarks which struck me as being totally devoid of sympathy or understanding; in fact the sort of advice one's own relations might wish to give one, but were tactful enough not to do so! Also I was furious that a complete stranger should dare to call my beautiful boat 'that old tub'. However, whether we liked it or not, the petty officer had decided to act as a sort of nanny-cum-governess to us: in fact, he would hardly let us out of his sight all evening because, he warned us, we might be molested by a party of drunks returning to their ship.

Early next morning a proud Haggis appeared at the top of the ladder bearing a fine specimen of mahogany planking over one shoulder. No one enquired where he had found it, but there were several pairs of willing hands to help expedite its stealthy descent on to the *Rumania*'s after deck. In case the skipper should feel inclined to criticize it in any way, Haggis bawled at him from above; 'Ye'll nae find sich a bonny wee plank onywhere betwixt here an' Gleska, mon!'

Captain Griffiths paid no attention, but it was clear that the wood met with his approval for he knelt on the deck and began to draw curious hieroglyphics on it with the stub end of a pencil.

Winkle was busy cleaning the navigation lamps and filling them with paraffin, but I had nothing much to do and felt restless and frustrated at not being able to cross to France for our time was running short, and we should soon have to revise our plans and return to London instead. To make matters worse the wind had dropped and the sea was calm and blue-green—a perfect summer's day. It looked as if the making of the new rudder might prove to be a lengthy business, but I did not like to ask the skipper exactly *how* long, for I was fully aware of our extraordinary good fortune in finding someone who had volunteered to help us in that marvellous way. But I could not settle down, so I hung around on the deck of the tug getting under Captain Griffith's feet and generally making a nuisance of myself.

'For God's sake get out of my sight, woman!' he roared at me after a few minutes. 'Go and get lost up on the cliffs for the rest of the day, or you'll have to wait till kingdom come for your blasted rudder!'

Haggis and his mates made extravagant gestures of sympathy at me from behind the skipper's back but Winkle, who had finished the lamps by then, whispered; 'Better take his advice, hadn't we?'

After a long steep climb we found ourselves on a chalky footpath high above the Camber Dock. We set off towards the northeast, sometimes dipping into valleys filled with the scent of summer flowers, and at other times scrambling upwards over the ridges where the fields of shimmering corn swayed dizzily under the August sun. There were crickets chirruping in the long grass and a few drowsy seagulls conversing in gentle twitters on the cliff-face. And away to the east a never-ending pageant of shipping steamed up and down the Dover Strait.

At last we came to the South Foreland and sat down to rest below the great white lighthouse. It seemed to me the most beautiful place I had ever seen and suddenly I knew, without a shadow of doubt, that I should come back there to live one day.

We returned to the Camber late that evening to find that Captain Griffiths had finished our new rudder and it had already been shipped, so there was nothing to stop us from crossing to France. But we were tired after our long walk and slept until late the following morning, by which time the wind had risen again. It blew a southerly gale for the next three days, so the *Imp* and I had to wait another year before our second attempt to cross the Channel.

3. TO SEA IN A SIEVE

'If you want my private opinion,' said Margaret, focussing the binoculars with some care; 'that's the whistle buoy on the Ridens de Calais!'

'Yes, I know,' I lied cheerfully. 'I decided to change course in mid-Channel so that we could reach France much sooner, in case the engine breaks down.'

'What a splendid idea!' Margaret smiled serenely and gave me one of her understanding looks. We were speeding triumphantly towards our first French buoy after three hours at sea aboard the *Imp* and, not unnaturally, it came as a complete surprise to discover that we were outside the port of Calais when I had laid off a direct course from Dover to Dunkerque! But at least it was France which loomed ahead—that hump of land on the starboard bow and the low sand-dunes disappearing into the hazy distance away to port—and the sea was sapphire and gold, shimmering under the hot July sun, with only the gentlest of ripples slapping against our clinker-built hull.

Margaret Boggis was an old friend from my seafaring days in the W.R.N.S. We had met on the same stoker's course in Portsmouth, and later worked together on the Captain's launch at H.M.S. *Abatos*, our first base in Southampton. She had already achieved First Class Honours in Classics at Oxford before joining the W.R.N.S., and for the past three years she had been teaching at Cheltenham Ladies' College.

Despite our diversion via the Ridens de Calais, we were picking our way through the wilderness of wrecks outside Dunkerque only six hours after leaving Dover. Motoring past the tall lighthouse at the harbour entrance was one of the proudest moments of my life: the *Imp* had finally crossed the Channel without mishap and arrived in her very first foreign port.

'*Bonjour*, Mees!' exclaimed a hoarse, bibulous voice associated with a big square fishing-net on one side of the Avant Port. 'You 'ave kom from where?'

'*Angleterre, Monsieur!*' I shouted happily at the fishing-net, which began to plunge up and down in an excitable manner.

'*Ce n'est pas vrai! Dans ce petit sabot? Mais je vois seulement deux jeunes filles–ou est le capitaine . . . le pilote?*'

The fisherman abandoned his net to sit on a bollard above the *Imp* so that he could peer inside the cabin and drink in all the details, at the same time continuing his questionnaire. Dressed in faded blue dungarees with a black beret pulled rakishly over one eye, he exuded a totally French aroma of Gaulloise Bleu, raw garlic and Pernod.

Presently Margaret spread our red and white check tablecloth over the engine casing and laid the table for supper. By the time it was ready our fisherman friend had rounded up a throng of *copains* who were jostling each other for orchestra stalls on the jetty high above us.

I emerged from the cabin bearing a saucepan of Scotch broth, and had just started pouring it into our soup bowls when something cold and clammy hit me on the left ear. I began to swear, then noticed that Margaret was doubled up with laughter and a noise like gale-driven surf had erupted from a score of open mouths above us. Two seconds later the cold wet thing swung past the end of my nose, paused for a moment, then began to jerk up and down over our supper table. At last it dawned on me that we were being offered a giant plaice with which to celebrate our first evening in France!

An hour later we sat blissfully replete on either side of the cockpit, listening to the murmur of Franco-Flemish voices relaying the details of our voyage, with numerous exciting embellishments, to the latest arrivals who had come to swell the throng.

'*Vive la France!*' cried Margaret, raising her can of lager skywards.

Several bottles of vin ordinaire shot up to answer her toast, and a gnarled old fisherman with a far-away gaze proposed; '*Vive les jolies filles d'Angleterre!*'

Out towards the harbour entrance we could see the funnels and masts of wrecked ships leaning at crazy angles against the setting sun, and there was one very bright star twinkling above the townhall spire.

* * * * *

Leaving Dunkerque with the fair tide next morning, we motored steadily eastwards past the sandbanks bordering the Zuydcoote Pass and the famous beaches which were still littered with wrecks. I closed my eyes for a second and saw the thousands of soldiers huddled together among the sand-dunes, the German planes swooping low over the coastline, bombs exploding everywhere and the little boats from England heading in towards the beaches.... Suddenly it occurred to me that the *Imp* might have been there before, one of that splendid fleet of rescue ships which crossed to France in 1940.

After Zuydcoote we motored on into Belgium waters, past all the straight-up-and-down seaside resorts, the inviting harbour entrances of Nieuport and Ostende, and the great mole at Zeebrugge. The *Imp* rounded the end of the mole some six hours after leaving Dunkerque and, making for a sheltered corner of the fishing harbour, we moored alongside another English boat called *Daydream*.

Margaret and I turned in early that night and slept soundly until just before dawn, when I awoke with a start. Fractionally opening one eye I saw one of my plimsolls float past the bunk in the half-light, like a semi-submerged log drifting upstream on the flood. I put out a hand and, horror of horrors, it was not just a bad dream; the water had almost reached the level of our bunks.

'You *did* mention in your invitation that she was rather a

leaky boat!' murmured Margaret drowsily, as we rolled out of our sleeping-bags and started baling for dear life.

After an hour's hard work we had reduced the water level to just below the deck-boards and I began to grovel around on my hands and knees in the dank cold cockpit, searching for the cause of that drastic new leak. I put my head under the stern thwart and a gush of oily bilge-water rose up to meet me, drenching my pyjamas and doing nothing to improve my early morning temper.

'Bring the torch quickly,' I shouted over my shoulder; 'I think I've found it at last!'

Wrenching up the deck-boards, I shone the light on the stern gland and saw a steady stream of water pouring through a thumb-sized hole in the sternpost. I stuck my thumb into the hole and sat there shivering in the cold fishy dawn, while Margaret pumped for another half hour then changed places with me.

By breakfast-time the bilges were empty and the sun had risen, but we could not decide whether to stay in Zeebrugge and hunt for a shipwright or try to reach Holland first. Fortunately Commander Thatcher, the charming owner of *Daydream*, came across to examine our leak at that juncture and helped to make up our minds for us. He filled the hole with cotton-waste coated with thick grease as a temporary measure, and promised to keep an eye on us out at sea; the weather was still fine and Flushing only fifteen miles away, so we decided to make a dash for Holland and hope for the best.

The voyage to Flushing was calm and uneventful, apart from the nagging anxiety about our leak which required constant supervision, some strange rumbling noises inside the engine and a brush with a round black object in the Schelde estuary which looked suspiciously like a drifting mine.

Our first Dutch windmill soon appeared above the sea-wall at Flushing, and there were many large merchant ships anchored off the town. It was my first sight of Walcheren Island and I found it strangely exciting—the sweep of the sand-dunes away towards Westkapelle, the lovely old church tower of St Jacob's rising above the oldest part of the town and a mighty flood tide racing past the harbour entrances.

We waved goodbye to our friends on *Daydream* who were

sailing on up the Schelde, and motored into the great sea-lock at Flushing where we moored alongside a pilotage vessel. Margaret, who was busy making fast our bow-line, smiled sweetly at the Dutch pilot on the other end of the line and said; '*Dank U wel, Mijnheer. Hoe ver is het van hier naar Vere, als't U blieft?*'

She was answered by a huge grin and a deluge of long guttural words from several men who had suddenly appeared on deck. Quite unruffled, she extracted a little book entitled *Dutch in Six Easy Lessons* from the pocket of her bell-bottomed trousers and began to ask them detailed questions about the canals in Holland.

'You never told me that you could speak Dutch?' I remarked rather jealously, once we had cleared customs and passed through the lock.

'I've never tried before!' she laughed. 'But I wouldn't dream of visiting a new country without being able to utter a word.'

We passed through another lock, pumping desperately all the time, as Commander Thatcher's grease had worn rather thin by then. Presently we found ourselves on the Middelburg Canal which runs right across Walcheren Island to the ancient village of Veere on the north-east coast. We motored past long canal barges with baby's play-pens on their foredecks and miniature flower gardens round their sterns; the bargees waved gaily and the tranquil Dutch landscape slid by on either hand. I could see black and white cows grazing in the fields, and women on bicycles wearing flowing black skirts and white lace bonnets; and then the great townhall of Middelburg rising our of a sea of red-tiled roofs. Another four miles with the scent of sun-kissed farmland wafting towards us on the northerly breeze; and suddenly there was Veere, just like I had always hoped it would be . . . the most beautiful village in the whole wide world.

There are four conspicuous landmarks in Veere—the church, townhall, hotel and windmill. Seen from a distance on a misty day they float in the air like some celestial vision, seemingly detached from the village beneath them. In the fourteenth century Veere was a flourishing seaport carrying on a brisk trade in woollen goods with Scotland. The harbour could hold seventeen merchant ships but, tragically, its prosperity vanished overnight during a terrible storm in the seventeenth century when most of the town was destroyed by floods. However, the gigantic church, built in 1348, stood its ground and was later used as a hospital by Napoleon's soldiers while he himself made his headquarters in the little fortress, now a hotel, guarding the harbour entrance. By the twentieth century Veere had become a peaceful fishing village, the haunt of artists and authors, with certain inexplicable magic properties which cast a spell over most people who ventured to land there.

We turned a sharp corner out of the canal exit into the East Schelde just as the townhall clock struck four, followed by a melodious carillon of bells. As if this was a signal to enter the tiny fishing harbour, I noticed a long line of black fishing-boats, pursued by hundreds of squawking gulls, speeding towards the narrow entrance. The quayside below the hotel was packed with smiling chattering women wearing their old Zeeland costumes, and the whole scene was so enchanting that I rubbed my eyes to make sure that I was not dreaming.

Suddenly aware of the strong tidal stream rushing us past the harbour, I advanced the throttle to full ahead and we sped between the ancient wooden jetties and past the clamorous shrimp-boats, until we came to rest alongside a small Belgian fishing-boat called *Hjordis*.

It had been a long hard day, what with the constant pumping and worries about our leak and engine, the perilous navigation in the Schelde estuary, and our first experience of working a boat through busy locks and avoiding collisions on a narrow canal. Suddenly the reaction set in and Margaret glared unhappily at the bilge-pump and said, 'What shall we do now? The *Imp* will soon sink at this rate.'

'Don't worry,' I tried to sound optimistic. 'Just sit down and have some tea and someone's sure to help us.'

'Why on earth should they?' Margaret had a much more logical outlook than me. 'You surely don't expect to find someone like Commander Thatcher every night, do you?'

'You wait and see,' I advised her without much conviction. I was never any good at countering the clear-headed reasoning with which she tackled all her problems.

After tea we went ashore and walked rapidly round the village in search of a boat-building yard. But it was Saturday evening and everywhere was closed; each door-step had its quota of large, medium and tiny pairs of clogs, announcing the presence of their owners within. We wandered gloomily back to the *Imp*, hardly aware of the haunting beauty of the fourteenth-century houses and miniature townhall overlooking the tranquil harbour.

'Allow me to present myself—François Bernard of the Brussels' theatre!' A tall handsome man arose from *Hjordis* cockpit, clearly playing the part of Don Quixote as he ushered us aboard with a sweeping gesture of his right arm.

Suddenly the gloom dispersed and the magic of Veere began to cast its spell about us. François took us in hand immediately, and as he knew everyone in Veere, less than an hour had passed before a local shipwright came to make arrangements for slipping the *Imp* on the next high water.

At five o'clock on Sunday morning the endearing François woke us with mugs of tea, and shortly afterwards we moved the *Imp* on to the grid at the far end of the harbour. As soon as the tide had dropped sufficiently the shipwright put a copper patch on the outside of the hull, then cut out the rotten wood in the stern-post and replaced it with some seasoned oak which he assured us would last for years. The bill for several hours' work came to less than fifteen shillings.

During our morning on the slip we made the acquaintance of Henk von Cranenburgh, a young man from Delft who had sailed into Veere harbour soon after the war and fallen in love with the place. He bought the old fortress on the harbour entrance and was busy transforming it into a very beautiful small hotel. Already the bar and dining-room were filled with his treasures—models of old Dutch sailing-barges, prints and seacapes of Zeeland, ship's lanterns hanging by the windows in the round tower, Delft plates and tiles on the walls and antique brass candlesticks on the dining-room tables.

That evening Margaret and I sat at a table near the west window eating smoked eels and watching the seals playing on the sandbanks out in the Veregat. The sun went down behind the windmill and there were ruby and gold reflections in the still waters of the harbour. I knew next to nothing about the magic of Veere in those days, and did not realize that already I was a helpless captive, like a shrimp inside a net: nor did I imagine that Henk would become a lifelong friend, and the magnetic influence of that obscure Dutch fishing village would pull my boat across the North Sea, year after year.

A great peace had descended on the sleeping harbour when Margaret and I strolled back to the *Imp*. Not a halliard stirred nor a leaf rustled along the fish quay, and high up above us the golden galleon weathercock on the townhall spire was conversing with Castor and Pollux, the Heavenly Twins.

We left Veere early next morning and rounded the western end of Noord Beveland just as the young flood came roaring in from the North Sea. Suddenly we were in the middle of a Ruisdael seascape—thunder and lightning, then hailstones, torrents of rain and brilliant shafts of sunlight streaming through the heavy black cumuli, with foaming waves rampaging across a pair of sinister sandbanks called Onrust and Hompels. I looked back at the delicate silhouette of Veere, but immediately my gaze was transfixed by the size of the following seas building up in the Roompot and I was nearly swept overboard by a vicious wave which exploded under the port quarter.

Our main leak had certainly been eliminated, but the *Imp*'s hull tended to open up like a basket each time it was exposed to a rough sea. What with the constant pumping and exciting navigation in the broad estuary of the East Schelde, there was always plenty to worry about. During the brief intervals when the bilges were empty, despite all the tumult around us, Margaret sat calmly on the engine cover reading out historical details about Zierikzee, the oldest village of Zeeland, which we could already see on the northern horizon.

Much to our dismay, the carburettor suddenly started making unhealthy popping noises. We struggled on for another hour, then decided to turn into Zijpe, a place described as a *Vluchthaven* on the chart, which Margaret proudly translated as 'Refuge Harbour'.

We moored alongside *Lutza*, a small Dutch sailing-boat owned by a stalwart red-faced man in a khaki shirt and trousers who surprised no one when he introduced himself as Colonel Steenkamp of the Dutch army. His crew was the complete contrast . . . an artistic member of the Diplomatic Service, he was clad in a black beret, a canary-yellow pullover and sky-blue dungarees; at a later stage he confided to Margaret that philosophy and foreign affairs were his specialities, but *not* sailing.

No sooner had we secured our mooring lines and springs to the Colonel, than the barge on the other side of *Lutza* indicated its urgent desire to leave harbour. The Colonel's engine refused to start, so we offered him a tow while the barge manoeuvred away from the jetty. Violent gusts of wind blew the pair of us rapidly down towards the wooden piles, and Colonel Steenkamp roared at his companion to place fenders on the starboard side and to lasso a bollard high up above the drifting boats. The crew leapt energetically around amid a vast tangle of ropes, missed the bollard three times but nearly hooked his skipper instead, then partially disappeared over the side but saved himself by grabbing one of *Lutza*'s flimsy wire stays, which began to twang like a hysterical violin string. The Colonel, who nourished a violent contempt for anyone who was not boat-minded, uttered a frightful word which sounded to our unaccustomed ears like '*Verflooschtestroomfolploogehund*'; simultaneously he rushed for'ard with a coil of rope and finally managed to secure us to the jetty.

After all those excitements there followed a period of peace and tranquillity. The wind was blowing gale force by then, so we decided to remain in Zijpe for the time being. I changed the oil in the *Imp*'s sump, and the diplomat borrowed Margaret's travelling mirror to facilitate his evening toilette before going out to dinner in a neighbouring inn.

A belt of torrential rain moved in over Zeeland that night. Our skylight leaked persistently, so that we were obliged to sleep with basins and saucepans balanced on top of our sleeping-bags to prevent them from becoming saturated. The *Imp*'s cabin was like the inside of a car-wash; always some water squirting at you from one direction or another.

Our voyage across Zeeland that summer often reminded me of *The Pilgrim's Progress*. There were no yacht marinas and very few yachts in those far off days just after the war, and the dams between the islands had not yet been conceived. With the strong tides rushing in across the shifting sandbanks, navigation was often an exciting challenge and the temperamental behaviour of the engine all added to the uncertainty of our existence. Each new day was filled with moments of exasperation and despair, and other moments of wonder and delight. But there was one constant factor about which we had no doubts; the people who manned the working boats of Zeeland—the coasters, shrimp-boats, tugs and barges—were our guardians and our friends.

We left Zijpe early next morning, bound for Dordrecht. Some two hours later, near the entrance to a narrow channel most aptly called the Hellegat, we hastily revised our plans because of the size of the waves crashing into the cockpit, which had a disastrous effect on the engine. Thankfully turning away from that vile stretch of water where the wind funnels down at one from three directions at once, we made for another *Vluchthaven* called Dintelsas. Inside the harbour there was a Dutch barge, the *Willem Barents*, run by an old skipper and his pretty daughter with twenty boys and girls as their passengers, and they invited us to moor the *Imp* alongside them.

'Vat is de trouble?' asked the barge skipper, peering under the engine cover as if he expected to find a nest of adders installed on the cylinder head. 'Aha!' he suddenly exclaimed with deep feeling: '*Jan, kan U kommen?*'

A few minutes later our carburettor, magneto, water-pump and petrol filter lay in small pieces on the deck of the barge, while a dozen budding mechanics tinkered with them and shouted at one another under the stern surveillance of the skipper. I was rather worried until the engine had been reassembled and started up when, much to everyone's surprise and delight, it ran quite sweetly with no further murmurs of protest.

We spent a very happy evening aboard the *Willem Barents*, talking and singing with the skipper and his lively crew to the accompaniment of a pianist and a trombonist. It was to be our last relaxed evening for some days, as we were beginning to run short of time.

* * * * *

Amsterdam was our goal, the Mecca towards which we were struggling with all our will power; but it took us another four days to get there owing to long delays at railway bridges and certain locks, as well as further engine trouble.

We crept precariously through Dordrecht in the dark, then on past the great shipbuilding yards on the Oude Maas. Rotterdam was like a nightmare. Freighters, tugs and barges rushing at one from all directions, with mountainous washes following in their wake; then the mighty Willemsbrug with the tide sluicing past its piers, followed by a frantic search for the right aperture, before we were swept irrevocably past it, to lead us into the Delft Canal.

We motored through Central Holland in a heat-wave, wearing sun-hats fashioned from out-of-date charts clenched together at the corners with safety-pins. First there was beautiful Delft and Leiden, then the shining Kaagmeer where hundreds of sailing dinghies circled around us like butterflies on a summer's day. The calm waters of the lakes and canals lulled us into a state of false security—no more leaks nor engine trouble; everything serene and peaceful from then onwards.

Sometimes the bridges were just high enough for us to pass beneath without summoning a bridge-keeper, but Margaret usually lay on the cabin-top with a tape-measure as we approached some doubtful arch and shouted 'full astern' when she judged it too low. However, on one occasion we stuck firmly underneath the bridge, with only a small section of the cockpit still visible to the excited populace who had gathered like bees round a honey-pot.

'Please do come aboard,' Margaret enticed them in her best Dutch. 'We need at least six people!'

A few seconds later the *Imp* had sunk well below her normal water-line, with ten of the heaviest citizens of Leidschendam dispersed throughout the cabin and cockpit.

'Bravo!' exclaimed a broad-shouldered postman, as the boat began to inch forward. '*Wij gaan direct door naar England?*'

There were cheers and roars of laughter, and we had some difficulty in disembarking our willing cargo on the far side of the bridge.

The run along the North Sea Canal into Amsterdam was quite as terrifying as our passage through Rotterdam. Leaving the *Imp* in Sixhaven, an extremely smart yacht harbour where she looked like a sparrow among a colony of pedigree doves, we took a busman's holiday in a sleek glass-roofed water-bus which toured the city, then treated ourselves to a four-course meal in a pretty old inn. Returning to the *Imp* later that night, I noticed that our Red Ensign had been taken down and placed under the stern thwart.

Originally we had planned to stay in Amsterdam for a few days before setting off on the long journey home. But, as often happens on a boat, we were running short of time; and a visit from a blasé yachtsman who behaved as if he owned Sixhaven helped to precipitate our departure. Referring to the *Imp* as 'that old tub', he asked if the engine was tied together with string, and expressed his astonishment that we had ever reached Amsterdam at all! Then he peered offensively through the open skylight and wished to know how we managed to navigate without a chart-table and where the water-closet was concealed? Ignoring his presence, I spread our chart of the Zuyder Zee on the engine cover and layed off some courses; then we cast off our lines and motored thankfully out of Sixhaven.

It was a sparkling blue and silver day on the Zuyder Zee, and we skimmed across the dancing waves to the little island of Marken. Multi-coloured reflections from the painted wooden houses clustered round the harbour came rippling towards us, and all the people, even the harbourmaster, wore their national costumes. It was like a scene from a Hans Andersen fairy-tale, and I pictured the *Imp* as a magic boat which had come to rescue a captive prince from the clutches of some evil old sea-witch!

* * * * *

We started back home that same afternoon, as there were only seven days left until the end of our holiday. Selecting another route south via Alphen and Gouda, we motored through a gentle landscape of flower-filled meadows and small canals lined with tall reeds which concealed families of ducks and moorhens. The long barges sped by in a flurry of windswept washing and smiling children, who waved and shouted to us from their wheel-house windows.

Later on there was the din of the great shipbuilding yards of Rotterdam and Dordrecht, and a few hours alongside *Lutza* in the little harbour of Willemstad. By the following evening we were back in the real heart of Zeeland, among the lonely purple sandbanks inhabited by gulls, cormorants and seals. The sun went down in a blaze of glory over Noord Beveland and a police-launch chased us across the East Schelde into the Zuid Beveland Canal.

'*Waar is de stern licht?*' demanded our pursuers, as we entered the lock together.

'Broken, I regret!' I spread out my oily hands with a gesture of helplessness; meanwhile Margaret offered round our last box of chocolates and established a congenial atmosphere by praising the speed of their launch in Dutch.

It was dark and very windy by the time we reached Hansweerd at the other end of the canal. We crossed the West Schelde to Terneuzen, and waited there for several hours until the turn of the tide. At 2 a.m. we set off into the cold black night and crept downstream on the first of the ebb. All around us were ghostly sandbanks, flashing red, white and green buoys, ships of all sizes on the move and shooting stars in the sky above.

'Very exciting' I wrote in the log-book after our dawn arrival off Flushing. 'Wet and beastly!' was added near Zeebrugge some three hours later, after a vile struggle to windward amid green breaking seas which threatened to swamp us.

The *Imp* was leaking badly again by then, the wind was rising all the time and Margaret and I were very tired. 'Enough is enough' we said, or something equally profound, and turned into the canal which runs south to Bruges, then west behind the coastline into France.

Travelling in company with *Sparkling Seas*, a little English yacht crewed by three large men with an equally large fog-horn —very important if you wish to make progress along the Belgian canals—we reached the frontier post at Ghyvelde the following afternoon. The first French bridge-keeper was having a postprandial siesta and had to be roused from his bed.

'*Vite! vite! Espèce de tortue*,' he roared at me as I struggled to restart the engine. Margaret, who had already anticipated this contingency, was running along the tow-path with the bow-line over one shoulder, hauling the *Imp* behind her.

On the outskirts of Dunkerque a big crowd lined the canal banks on either hand, clearly in a festive mood for they waved and shouted and blew kisses to us, and some even offered bottles of wine. Margaret and I behaved like royalty, bowing, smiling and waving, first to one side then the other.

'How sweet of them to give us such a splendid welcome!' beamed my companion as we sped on into the industrial quarter of the city. Later we were told that an international cycling race, led by the French champion, was expected in Dunkerque that afternoon; but the cycle king was late and we came first, which explained the warmth of our reception!

We left Dunkerque at the wrong time next day as there was no way of escaping from the canals via the sea-lock until the *Twickenham Ferry* was due to sail. Because of this we were obliged to stem the tide for five hours and watch the sea building up with a freshening westerly wind.

Margaret and I tied ourselves into the cockpit with the mooring lines, and steered towards the setting sun. The tiller had developed a will of its own, and the compass needle spun round and round in crazy circles; luckily I knew roughly where England lay! It was a crossing which lacked all charm, what with the waves breaking into the cockpit every few seconds and the *Imp* rolling alarmingly in the big beam seas. We took it in turns to pump continuously and, for once, the engine never faltered—perhaps it was pleased to be on its way home.

Margaret was completely encased in oilskins and Balaclava helmet, apart from a pair of laughing green eyes above a very sunburnt nose: whenever I looked at her I felt reassured, and momentarily less aware of our dismal surroundings. It was she who first saw England—just a faint hint of coastline in the gathering twilight—then the three great beams from the South Foreland Lighthouse suddenly came sweeping across the sea to welcome us home.

After a ten and a half hour passage, we felt like conquering heroes that night as we sped through the eastern entrance of Dover Harbour and waved to the man high up in the signal station.

'Where are you from?' he bellowed at us through his loud-hailer.

'Amsterdam!' I shouted at the top of my voice.

* * * * *

The *Imp* won the Hurlingham Yacht Club's trophy for the boat which had made the longest voyage that year. I received a small silver shield at the Annual Dinner, and a sextant, to be kept for one year only, with my name engraved on the brass plaque fixed to the lid of the box. That sextant completely went to my head! I had no idea how to use it, but suddenly I pictured myself as a famous Master Mariner taking meridian altitudes, star sights and amplitudes a thousand miles from the land. I used to pose in front of the mirror, trying to imitate the stance of a professional navigator as portrayed in Captain Watts' little book, *The Sextant Simplified* . . .

The following summer I took the sextant with me aboard a small Norwegian steamer on which my parents and I were making a voyage to the Arctic Circle. The Captain, seeing my treasured box on deck one day, invited me up on the bridge to shoot the evening stars. The Mate and Second Mate were there too, with their sextants aimed like machine-guns at those tiny quivering fireflies which I could not even *find* in my telescope, let alone bring them down to some obscure line between the sea and the sky.

'Shoot!' roared the Captain, with his eyes glued to the chronometer. I twiddled the micrometer head and prayed that no one was watching me.

'Now you vill vork out your readings, yuist like the Mate, and tell me the answers, yes?' said the Captain, after my fourth star had been annihilated in a blue-black sea.

That was the one thing which I really could *not* do, so I fixed the Second Mate with a look of desperation; already he had taught me how to make a monkey's fist out of an old bit of manilla rope. He signalled to me to wait for him on the lower deck when he came off watch.

Half an hour later I leant on the guard-rail looking out to sea, towards the dark skerries floating in the twilight haze and the tiny lighthouses flashing their warning signals across the calm waters. Suddenly they disappeared, and in their place a large red apple dangled in front of my eyes, suspended by a length of cod-line from the deck above.

'This doesn't look like the prelude to a lesson in astronavigation!' I thought to myself. 'But never mind; I'll learn how to use a sextant one day if it's the last thing I do on earth.'

I took a bite of the apple just as my father appeared on deck.

'It's time for our game of chess,' he said, studiously ignoring a scene which had many of the ingredients of the Garden of Eden in reverse.

4. SINGLE-HANDED PASSAGE

I cannot remember a time when I definitely *wanted* to become a single-handed sailor. The rare specimens I had met seemed churlish individuals—completely self-centred with a marked preference for their own company above all other, and a constant preoccupation with their own news value. There were, of course, the odd rather splendid ones, ardently searching for their Golden Fleece which drove them on and on, despite all their fears and loneliness. But I had no such incentive, nor any special desire to go solo-voyaging in the *Imp*.

Two years after my first voyage to Holland I was, however, forced into the single-handed role by a series of events over which I had no control: Margaret was teaching in Kenya High School by then; Sue was married with a baby on the way, and Winkle could spare only a few days that summer during which time we brought the *Imp* from London round to Dover. Best friends, who were prepared to endure the rigours of a holiday afloat, were becoming harder to pin down each year. It *did* sometimes occur to me that they might have been tempted by a safer and more comfortable boat, but I soon dismissed such tedious thoughts as irrelevant nonsense.

I had managed to lure another old friend, Daphne Napper, into spending a week of her short annual holiday with me that summer. She had never set eyes on the *Imp* before, nor had she any previous boating experience to prepare her for whatever was in store for us. I felt rather guilty about the whole arrange-

Single-handed Passage

ment, remembering my cousin, Bunty, and the vows I had made that awful night on the Maplin Sands; also my mother, who kept a watchful eye on my summer boating plans, was being left in ignorance of the exact length of time Daphne and I would be together aboard the *Imp*.

A week of gales preceded the chosen day for our departure. The Dover Strait was churned up into a cauldron of tumbling waves and a harbour-bound mariner, who was comfortably secured in a corner of the Wellington Dock, stressed that we should find the sea much calmer if we made our crossing at night. Following his advice, we left Dover at midnight. About five miles out from the English coast the log-book records: 'Full moon, heavy ice-cold dew and even heavier swell! Channel stuffed with shipping.'

I went into the cabin to put on an extra jersey and tap the barometer, hoping, rather unkindly, that our adviser was having nightmares in his snug sleeping-bag in Dover. I had not been gone for more than two minutes when Daphne cried out, 'There are some brilliant red and green lights very close to us— do you think they're quite all right?'

I bounded back into the cockpit and rammed the tiller hard over to port, just in time to prevent the *Imp* from being pulverised by an enormous freighter which came rushing at us out of the night. After her wash, which nearly capsized us, had finally died down, we poured out two large tumblers of rum and orange and drank a toast to Father Neptune!

Apart from that alarming episode, Daphne's week passed most happily. There was Dunkerque in the dawn haze; the peaceful Belgian fishing harbour of Nieuport with dinner *chez* Madame De Wit-Verplancke, the kindly patronne of a bargee's café with whom I had made friends the previous summer; then another run in a big quartering sea to Zeebrugge, followed by a gale which we weathered most comfortably in a sheltered corner of the inner harbour. On Daphne's last evening we sailed into the Schelde estuary with a huge red sun dipping behind the soft grey horizon astern. It was one of those moments, which are not uncommon at sea, when you drift along in a timeless world of intense beauty and all the problems of the land are swept aside in the sudden clarity of your perception.

There was a letter awaiting Daphne in Flushing from her boyfriend, which gave a clear picture of the anguish he was suffering while she braved the perils of the North Sea. She became engaged to him soon after her return to England, and they have now been happily married for a good many years. I always like to think that the *Imp* played a small part in helping them to make up their minds.

Just before Daphne left Flushing she hung over the stern-rail of the ferry and said, 'I feel so worried about you; I *do* hope you won't be desperately lonely, all on your own.'

I hoped so too. But suddenly I felt a few twinges of excitement at being a single-hander for the first time in my life.

* * * * *

There were plenty of hazards, I soon discovered, when navigating alone in a small motor-boat on the crowded Dutch rivers and canals. I began by making a valiant attempt to get myself efficiently organised: courses laid off on the charts before leaving harbour; hot soup in a Thermos and sandwiches cut directly after breakfast; engine maintenance carried out with more than usual fussiness, and the cockpit and cabin-top scrubbed until they shone. While under way I wrote up the log meticulously every hour, noted the barometer readings, wind direction and strength, and everything of interest I had passed; but there was no one else to keep a sharp look-out during the composition of those gems of maritime hyperbole, and within two hours of leaving Flushing I had a surprise encounter with a black and white heifer which suddenly loomed up fine on the starboard bow, nearly hit the railway bridge at Middelburg, and sliced some paint from the stern of a smart Belgian motor-cruiser whose owner called me something exceptionally unpleasant in Flemish.

Feeling thoroughly rattled and neurotic, I motored out of the Middelburg Canal determined to make a seamanlike entry into the fishing harbour at Veere. But I had forgotten to look up the direction of the tidal stream in the East Schelde, or to coil down my mooring lines which were heaped like grubby spaghetti on the foredeck and stern. It was spring tides, and the powerful stream caught the *Imp*'s stern just as I had reduced speed to negotiate the narrow entrance and spun her right round. Fortunately she was more 'in' than 'out' by then, so I advanced up the harbour stern first, trying to give the impression to everyone who was watching that this was my normal method of entering harbour. Henk, who had, by a stroke of ill luck, just appeared at a window of the Campveerse Toren, waved and shouted to me, his face contorted in a way that showed quite clearly how hard he was struggling not to hurt my feelings by exploding with laughter.

'Throw me your stern line,' barked the Commodore of the Hurlingham Yacht Club, who had, by some extraordinary coincidence, arrived in Veere that same afternoon.

'I can't! Try to catch me with your boat-hook,' I shrieked in desperation, as the tide swept the *Imp* swiftly past him while I tugged and cursed at the cat's cradle of rope.

He had strong arms, that Commodore, and he hauled me back alongside his yacht with the ease of an angler who finds a minnow on the end of his line.

'Come aboard and join us for tea,' invited his wife, when my lines were finally unravelled and secured. 'You look as if you've just crossed the Atlantic in stormy weather!'

The magic of Veere was stronger than ever that evening. I could just make out the faint outlines of the old houses through the gently swaying curtain of nets hung from the fishing-boat's masts to dry; and down by the harbour entrance a fisherman was playing some haunting tunes on his melodeon. The still water glowed with emerald, ruby and amber lights, and I could hear clogs clumping along the cobble-stoned quay mingling with the chimes of the townhall clock.

Leaving Veere next morning, I found the Schelde estuary in a friendly smiling mood. Low water among the sandbanks, with plump contented seals basking in the sunshine; botters and tjalks aground on the summits of purple ridges; a field of golden-yellow buttercups on Noord Beveland, and hundreds of tiny marsh birds singing their hearts out along the foreshore; windmills and church spires piercing the pale blue heavens above the dikes, and big bouncing buoys heeling eastwards, with the rampaging spring tide swirling past them. I grew to love those black and red buoys with their funny topmarks and flashing lights;

they seemed like old friends, always there to greet me at the various stages of my voyage, nodding or winking merrily as I motored past them.

A sheltered harbour in Noord Brabant was my next port of call. I selected my quarry, a small timber-barge, with some care and bore down upon it with fenders out and mooring lines neatly coiled and ready for use. Surprisingly everything went according to plan and the *Imp* was soon secured alongside the barge, whose aged skipper then sat down on a mound of logs and fixed me with a gaze of searching appraisal. He had glacier-blue eyes which were more accustomed to scanning the shining waterways than peering at floating females, and a thousand generations of male domination over the watery spaces of our earth made themselves felt in the guttural resonance of his voice.

'*Waar is de Kapitein?*' he demanded gruffly.

'*Ik ben de Kapitein,*' I replied rather nervously, in my best Dutch—how I wished that Margaret had been there to ease things along.

An expression of frank disbelief settled on the old man's rugged face, and as soon as he thought I was otherwise occupied he craned his neck forward and did a lightning reconnaissance of the inside of the cabin—no doubt he thought I was lying and had secreted the captain somewhere out of sight. His curiosity satisfied, he cut a plug of tobacco and chewed it thoughtfully for some minutes.

A small group of fishermen had collected on the jetty above us, and presently one of them took off his sabots and descended on to the barge. He and the skipper retired into the wheel-house to have a discreet confabulation, but I was constantly aware of their steady surveillance, despite the window-pane which now intervened.

After a short while the two sailors emerged, and the newcomer grasped my starboard shrouds with a bunch of fingers that resembled overripe bananas and shook the whole boat briefly to announce his intention to speak. It transpired that he was not unfamiliar with the English tongue and his friend, the barge skipper, had charged him with making a few enquiries.

'Vair do you kom from?' he asked, flashing me a brilliant smile.

'From Dover in England,' I proudly replied.

Single-handed Passage

'And you kom *alleen* over the *groot Noord Zee?*' he exclaimed excitedly.

I had met that question before, and it was always rather embarrassing as I felt obliged to explain that we had made the shortest possible sea crossing, then hugged the French and Belgian coasts so that we could dart into harbour if the weather showed signs of deteriorating. Luckily his English was strictly limited, and as he did not understand my reply I was able to bask in the glow of his admiration for my nautical prowess.

Next he wanted to know where I was bound for, and when I mentioned Rotterdam and said I hoped to get there quickly as time was running short, there was much nodding of heads and a further Dutch duologue took place.

An hour or so later I heard a knock on the cabin-top, and when I appeared the old barge skipper presented me with a beautiful polished wooden fid.

'Hendrik thees zelf-made had, and vill gif to you,' explained his friend, 'zo you kan maak vairy fine *splitsen*—how you say, "splices"?—with your ropes; and he hop you alzo maak vairy fine zelf-splice, zo you kom *niet alleen* over the *Noord Zee* nextime, O.K.?'

'O.K.,' I replied happily. 'I will use it very often and remember his wishes whenever I am splicing!'

I awoke with a start at five o'clock next morning, for there was a sound of rushing water sluicing past the hull and the *Imp* was shuddering from stem to stern. I leapt out into the cockpit to find that we were under way; Noord Brabant was rapidly fading into the dawn haze astern and my vessel was heading north-eastwards at about eight knots, still moored alongside the barge. Seeing my astonishment, old Hendrik came out of his wheel-house and offered me a steaming mug of coffee.

'*Goeden morgen*,' he greeted me, with a gleam of amusement illuminating his innocent blue eyes. Then he murmured something about a '*doorgaande boot naar Rotterdam*', which I took to mean that we were heading there, willy-nilly, at top possible speed!

* * * * *

I passed through much of the busiest part of Rotterdam under the wing of the old barge skipper. Casting me adrift just beyond the Willemsbrug, he indicated a timber wharf where he was going to unload his cargo.

I felt rather lonely after his departure, and a nervous wreck by the time I had manoeuvred through the various locks and bridges leading into the Delft Canal. Some two hours later I moored the *Imp* to a pair of trees bordering a quiet canal near the centre of the town, and went ashore for a stroll. In three hundred years, since the time when Jan Vermeer painted the peaceful canals reflecting those gems of seventeenth-century architecture and those glorious interiors inhabited by his timeless men and women, there have been very few changes in Delft and it is still one of the most enchanting towns in the whole of Holland.

Returning to the boat an hour or so later, I decided to have supper then go straight to bed, as I was already half asleep. After a brief spell inside the cabin—just long enough to heat my can of baked beans—I emerged into the cockpit to find six children and a well-nourished mongrel dog seated on the cabin-top. The eldest, a school-boy of about fourteen with tousled blond hair, a freckled face and large white teeth, introduced himself and his family with such charm of manner that I did not have the heart to suggest that they should go and play on someone else's boat.

By the end of my supper—and a week's supply of Black Magic chocolates—we had become friends for life and Leo, the eldest, said, 'You must now kom to our huis and take a koffie with our mother.'

Mother looked rather astonished when she saw what her children had dredged up from the neighbouring canal; nevertheless, she sat me down on a firmly-stuffed sofa with a lace antimacassar to protect the back, and in the fullness of time coffee and small sweet biscuits were served. The family sat round three sides of me, suddenly very demure and shy; while the fourth side was occupied by a selection of highly-polished green house-plants which regarded me in hostile silence. It is curious how *right* dirty unkempt seafarers feel at the end of a long day afloat, provided they adhere strictly to their own boat; and how abysmally *wrong*, if they should happen to find themselves in the middle of a Dutch provincial drawing-room!

Single-handed Passage

Next morning the children followed me on their bicycles for several miles, riding along the tow-path with their dog galloping behind them. By midday I was alone once more, and there followed a quiet period, socially, for the next six hours. I motored northwards under a leaden sky, through a cosy landscape of red-roofed farmhouses, immaculate fields, black and white cows, families of ducks and one marvellous heron.

I believe it was on the outskirts of Leiden, in the middle of a heavy downpour, that I first made the acquaintance of Jan Dorsman. His little sailing-boat, *Fidget*, nosed alongside the *Imp* during a wait at one of the bridges, and Jan cast his line and hooked me in one go by using the simplest bait in the world.

'What a beautiful boat you have!' he exclaimed, with the voice of one who really knows about boats. 'She must have a fine strong engine, has she not?'

After that, it was child's play for Jan. He attached his bow-line to the *Imp*'s stern cleat, introduced me to his Indonesian girl-friend who was lurking under the canopy which served as a cabin, and I towed *Fidget* along the canals of Central Holland for the next two days. It was by no means a one-sided arrangement, as Jan took us both out to supper in Leiden, and did all the hard work with the mooring lines whenever we stopped for bridges or locks to open.

'You should change your boat and learn how to sail,' he said rather tactlessly, during our farewell breakfast-party before our ways parted at the junction of the Ijssel and the Lek. 'You would find it a very beautiful experience and much more safe, *niet waar?* And on the canals you can always find a tow.'

'Like hell, you can!' I thought to myself. All the same he had sown a seed of uncertainty in my mind, as I had often envied that exclusive clan, the sailing-boat yachtsmen, who merely reefed their sails when the wind blew harder and never seemed to suffer from those miserable forebodings of disaster which cast a shadow over some of my finest days at sea. I longed to stifle that small insistent voice which invariably piped up; 'Whatever shall I do if the engine breaks down in really bad weather . . . ?'

The first few days of my return voyage were rather depressing. A combination of heavy rain, strong west winds and engine trouble reduced me to a state of dripping misery in which I failed to perceive the slightest beauty or romance in the stormy seascapes of Zeeland. On the third evening I traced the engine trouble to a dirty slow-running jet in the carburettor, and managed to cure it without immobilizing the whole engine. And not long afterwards I met a school of porpoises leaping ecstatically around in a sea of sparkling emeralds.

Despite the sudden change in my fortunes, yet another front was moving in—already I had noticed the high cirrus clouds in the western sky—and that glorious phosphorescent night could not last for ever. Being, perhaps, more than usually anxious not to meet a depression all by myself on the open sea, I turned into the Belgian canals at Zeebrugge.

The following day was hot, thundery and mosquito-ridden, with a great many bad-tempered fishermen concealed in clumps of reeds or beneath large black umbrellas, who arose and shook their fists at me each time the *Imp*'s propeller became entwined with one of their lines. I regretted my choice of route, and wished I had stuck to the open sea.

I met a tug with a long tow of barges—I believe there were six in all—at the bridge in the village of Plaschendaele. Presently her skipper sauntered along the tow-path to where the *Imp* was secured to a large stinking-nettle by a simple clove-hitch, and suggested to me; 'If Mademoiselle desires to attach herself to the ultimate barge, she will, without doubt, advance more rapidly and derange fewer bridge-keepers?'

I saw his point and it sounded an ideal arrangement as we would, in any case, be travelling in company as far as Nieuport, and my over-heated engine would have a chance to cool down. No sooner had the Plaschendaele Bridge opened and the tug with her tow of seven passed through, than a young man of startling good-looks of the Latin variety—a real *beau garçon*—emerged from under the hatch-cover of Barge No. 6, tweaked the *Imp*'s bow-line towards him and leapt nimbly on to the cabin-top.

'My name is Albert Bonaventure,' he announced with a fierce pride gleaming in his dark brown eyes, 'and I have come to keep you company in case you become *ennuyer* during the passage to Nieuport.'

Albert installed himself comfortably in the cockpit, declared that I was free to take his photograph if I desired, then suggested that I should prepare for him a light repast while he steered the *Imp*.

'How on earth shall I get rid of him this evening,' I thought to myself, as I laboured over the steaming-hot stove on that jungle-hot canal.

Luckily Madame De Wit-Verplancke was doing some crochet-work on the terrace of her café as the tug with its convoy pulled into the bank at Nieuport.

'Albert!' she boomed, in a voice like Flemish thunder. Then followed a string of incomprehensible words which reduced Monsieur Bonaventure to a whimpering pale-faced shadow of his former jaunty self. He hastily disappeared beneath the canvas which covered the hold of Barge No. 6, while Madame De Wit-Verplancke personally attached the *Imp*'s mooring lines to the lamp-posts outside her café and gave me a lecture on my lack of prudence in permitting such a scallywag to travel on my boat. Thoroughly chastened, I decided to return to the open sea at the earliest opportunity.

I left Nieuport at seven o'clock next morning. The sea was calm and blue, and there was not a cloud in the sky nor a breath of wind—where was that depression that had driven me inland, I wondered. The engine ran faultlessly and I sped past La Panne, Dunkerque and Gravelines with one foot dangling in the sea and the other one firmly wedged under the stern thwart. It was a lovely way to travel when the sun was hot; because the *Imp* had such a low free-board, I felt very much a part of the sea and closely—sometimes too closely—in touch with it.

I motored into Calais harbour about midday to wait for the west-going tide, and moored alongside a tug called *Courageux*.

'Perhaps Mademoiselle would like some *soupe à l'oignon* to fortify her for the *pleine mer*?' suggested the ship's cook, allowing me to catch a tantalizing whiff from under his saucepan lid. He was a man endowed with great sympathy and perception, and I set off for England soon after lunch in a most cheerful frame of mind. The soup had been accompanied by a tumbler of fiery *vin ordinaire*, with the result that I forgot to work myself up into a state of nerves about attempting my first single-handed

Channel crossing, and even viewed the waves breaking on the Ridens de Calais with a light-hearted nonchalance.

Three hours out from Calais I recorded in the log-book that there was a gentle swell and a thick white mist, with no coast in sight. By then the exhilarating effects of my lunch aboard the French tug had worn off, and been replaced by a deep sadness, tinged with pessimism; so this was what it felt like being in the middle of the Channel all by oneself in a fog . . . In actual fact I was *not* in the middle of the Channel, but in the middle of the south-bound shipping lane, which was far worse. All around me blared a dismal symphony of fog-horns, so I extracted my own tiny instrument from the cabin and blew what I judged to be one prolonged blast every two minutes.

'Might as well stick to the Rule of the Road,' I told myself gloomily, knowing full well that none of those big ships were ever likely to hear me.

From time to time I stopped the engine so that I could hear the thumping propellers and booming fog-horns more clearly, and listen for the diaphone on the South Goodwin Lightvessel. I had often heard it from the Dover cliffs—those two blasts every minute with a deep 'whoomph' at the end, which sounded so like a cow in pain; and I felt sure that I should recognize it out at sea. But it was disconcerting to find how distorted the noises had become in the fog, and how hard it was to retain any sense of direction: often I swung round to search for some immense vessel which seemed to be overtaking me at great speed, only to find that it had suddenly appeared a few cables away on the port bow; a mighty phantom ship stealing across the cold white sea. Everything I touched was cold and clammy, and dripping-wet, and my hair clung to the back of my neck like dank rat's tails.

I recalled some of the seafarers' tales about collisions and ships running aground on the Goodwin Sands; and I knew that fog was known to be one of the deadliest perils one could face at sea. But strangely enough, I did not feel lonely or frightened—not like I always felt when the wind blew harder and the sea became rough. Instead I had a curious sensation of peace, and a feeling of comradeship with all those phantom ships I seldom saw.

For some long while I had been sitting on the stern steering with great concentration, and peering alternately at the compass needle and the total blankness straight ahead; it was high time the English coast began to show up, fog or no fog. Suddenly I glanced upwards, and there were the soaring white cliffs of the South Foreland, their shoulders draped in gentle folds of sea-fog. It was the most beautiful sight I had ever seen.

An hour later the *Imp* was moored alongside a deserted fishing-boat in the Camber Dock in Dover; and I felt very humble and thankful to be safely home.

5. SHIPWRECK

The barometer had fallen dramatically in the past few hours—thirteen millibars since breakfast-time—and it now registered 949 millibars, the lowest I had ever seen it.

'Either it's gone crazy and just can't be relied on any more, or there's something quite extraordinary brewing up,' I told Winkle, after tapping it for the twentieth time.

'I believe they *do* sometimes go wrong,' she said, more to comfort me than with any real conviction. 'Anyway the sun's shining, the sea looks calm enough and it's only nine miles to Ostende.'

'All right; we'd better get going. The tide's been flooding for three hours so there should be enough water on the bar.' I swung the starting-handle and the engine roared into life.

We let go our mooring lines and motored out of the tiny harbour of Blankenberghe, past the deep draught fishing-boats still aground on the mud, the rickety wooden jetty leading to the small white lighthouse, the tall hotels and pensions preparing their evening meals, and the crowds of holiday-makers packing up their bathing-costumes and buckets and spades, ready to leave the beach. It was 5.30 p.m. on the ninth of August, and there was a light southerly breeze blowing off the shore; and, instinctively, I knew that I had made the wrong decision.

The *Imp* had been my boat for the past eight years, and during that time we had grown together like a pair of old shipmates who

Shipwreck

rely on one another for their driving force and *joie de vivre*. I knew all her faults and short-comings, and had compensated for most of them; and she, in her turn, had given me much happiness and looked after me in many tight corners. Each of us was incomplete without the other. Winkle, who knew the ways of boats and loved them dearly, understood all these things without a word being spoken.

The previous summer I had taken the *Imp* south for a change, exploring the Somme Bay and the coast of Normandy as far as Fécamp. But the urge to see Veere again had been too strong to resist after two whole years so I had been to Holland that summer, and Winkle came over to Flushing to join me for the last few days. We were now on our way home with a model of an old Zeeland shrimp-boat, carved by a Veere fisherman, stowed carefully under the starboard bunk.

Once we had cleared the shallow water close to the shore, the sea settled down into a long smooth swell and the *Imp* made good progress towards the west. It should not take us longer than two hours, I calculated, to reach Ostende on such a fine evening; one could hardly wish for a calmer sea or lighter wind . . . all the same, there was a hard green light in the northern sky which made me shiver.

'Look, there's the water-tower at Wenduine already,' said Winkle, pointing towards the south to distract my attention. 'And I do believe I can just make out the twin spires of Ostende Cathedral!'

I took the binoculars from her and steadied them on the rim of the cabin-top. Yes, that was Ostende without a doubt. Another seven and a bit miles and seventy minutes to go, and we should be there ourselves if all went well. We did not speak much after that. I pumped out the bilges and gave an extra turn to the grease-caps, and Winkle went into the cabin to fetch a warmer jersey, but I noticed her giving the barometer a surreptitious tap while she was inside.

We motored steadily west, about a mile off the shore, and it occurred to me that the beaches seemed strangely empty for the month of August—I supposed that everyone had gone home to supper. The city of Ostende grew larger every time I glanced over the port bow, and the water-tower at De Haan, which was already past our beam, reminded me of a tall grey mushroom. The gentle breeze from the south had backed round to the east, and I asked Winkle if she thought we should hoist the sail.

'There's only another two or three miles to go; we're off Spanjaard Duin now, and I can see the little church of St Theresia behind the sand-dunes,' she replied. 'I don't think it's worth the effort, do you?'

Before I had time to give the matter another thought, the light wind from astern dropped right away and I could no longer feel those small cold fingers drumming on the back of my neck.

'How strange,' I began . . . and then it hit me straight in the face—an icy brutal blast of wind which rapidly hardened, until it was blowing a howling gale out of the north-west. The harsh green light away to the north was transformed into an angry greenish-black cloud which came rushing towards us, whisking up the sea along its track. A few minutes later the waves looked like Himalayan peaks—I never realized these things could happen so quickly—and their towering white-crested summits came crashing aboard our poor little boat with her big open cockpit. The engine began to labour in the most alarming way; then, quite suddenly, it stopped. After that there was nothing but the roar of the wind in our flimsy shrouds and the thundering waves breaking on the beach.

Strange thoughts flashed through my mind during the long helpless minutes which ensued. I recalled in great detail some advice from my coastal navigation course about never allowing yourself to get caught on a lee shore; but if you *did* find yourself in that unfortunate position, you must head straight for the open sea and ride out the gale in deep water. Well, I knew that was impossible as the engine had broken down (later we discovered that the water-pump had split in two), and hoisting the sail would only help the wind to blow us faster on to the shore; and, in spite of the teachings of those Master Mariners which I had absorbed so conscientiously, I felt very relieved and thankful!

Voicing these unseamanlike thoughts, I shouted at Winkle, 'Thank God it's blowing us on to the beach and not out to sea! At least we should stand a chance of wading ashore.'

Shipwreck

'Better get the model fishing-boat out of the cabin before it's smashed up; also plenty of warm clothes,' she shouted back at me—it was quite hard to hear one another speak amid the din of the gale.

We drifted crabwise towards that seething inferno, with the cold merciless waves crashing into the cockpit every few seconds; by this time we were soaked to the skin and shivering uncontrollably.

'No good dropping the anchor,' I yelled at Winkle, noticing that she was trying to clamber on to the cabin-top. 'You'll only get swept overboard, and that rusty old chain wouldn't last for two seconds in this sea.'

We clung to the cockpit coaming and watched the shore advancing towards us—the military hospital, one mile from Ostende, on one side, and the little church of St Theresia on the other; and in the foreground that terrifying beach with the stone sea-wall behind it and a number of groynes set at right-angles to it, driving seawards into the welter of foam.

At last the *Imp* struck, and the full tragedy of what was happening to her began to dawn on me. Already she was beginning to pound on the hard sand ... what should we do next? I wanted to hide inside the cabin and cry my eyes out, but Winkle took charge and hauled me over the gunwale into the sea.

'Hold the fishing-boat above your head,' she screamed at me, 'and try not to trip over.'

The cold surf was up to our necks as soon as we let go the side of the boat and turned towards the shore. We struggled desperately to keep a foothold in that violent undertow, and I began to wonder if we should ever reach the shore. Suddenly a miracle took place—we were surrounded by soldiers in soaking-wet battledress who picked us up as if we were swansdown and carried us through the breakers on to dry land!

At last the great struggle was over and there was no need to think any more. They wrapped us up in dry blankets inside a candle-lit tent, and large men with kindly expressions on their faces circled round us, asking if there was anything else they could do. Already they had sent for the life-boat and the British Consul, given us large glasses of brandy and placed the model fishing-boat carefully down on a crate: my teeth were still chattering and the brandy began to go to my head—all I wanted was for someone to tell me that the *Imp* was safe—but I knew that was asking too much.

Presently the British Consul arrived—decidedly grumpy at being disturbed during his evening meal; and after he had cast an experienced eye over the pair of waterlogged and rather drunken British nationals served up for his dessert, he looked exceedingly melancholy.

'Better jump into the car,' he snapped, 'and I'll try to find a *pension* to take you in—not easy in the middle of August, you know—don't suppose you brought any money or passports ashore, did you?'

'No, nothing but this model,' I mumbled apologetically.

He glared malevolently at the Zeeland shrimp-boat, and would hardly allow us time to thank the group of commandos who had come to our rescue and done so much for us already. Just before we left their camp, the commanding officer promised to get in touch with the life-boat coxswain, who was still searching for us out at sea, and keep an eye on the *Imp* until high water, to try and stop her from pounding against the sea-wall.

The Consul's Belgian wife was very kind, and she managed to find lodgings for us in a small *pension* in the Rue de l'Yser; also she allowed us to use her telephone to ring up our families in England, and helped to make arrangements for the salvaging of the *Imp*.

The next few days dragged by like a terrible nightmare. We were both suffering from delayed shock and had no respectable clothes to wear; and our landlady regarded us with deep suspicion, obviously wondering who was going to settle her bill.

The onshore gale blew for three days without a break. Each morning, at low tide, Winkle and I returned to the *Imp* which had been cast up like a piece of drift-wood at the top of the beach. We would spend half the day crouching in the cockpit, ineffectually trying to shield the engine from the onslaught of sand which had found its way into every nook and cranny in the boat. And when the flood tide came roaring in we would move to a nearby groyne, praying that the strong anchor and chain which the life-boat coxswain had lent us would hold her stern in position and prevent her from hitting the sea-wall. Much to our regret, the commandos had finished their training among the sand-dunes and moved inland the morning after our stranding on the beach.

Arriving soon after breakfast on the third day, we found that the cabin door had been forced open and everything movable stolen: all the bedding, saucepans, mugs, plates and cutlery; even our faithful barometer and a plaque of the arms of Zeeland, given me by the Commodore of the Flushing Yacht Club, had been prized off the cabin bulkhead; and all the petrol had been drained from the tank. It was a bitter blow, and we decided to stay aboard until late that evening in case there were any other marauders about.

An hour or so before high water, just as the first angry waves began to surge around the outside of the hull, we noticed a number of men dressed more for the affairs of the city than a gale-swept beach, advancing towards the *Imp* with their trousers rolled up above their knees and their brief-cases held high against the drenching fusillade of spray. It was such an amazing sight that I felt like smiling for the first time in days; then one of them aimed a camera at us, and we realized that we were being confronted by the gentlemen of the press!

On the day that we hit the headlines—'Two Englishwomen Fight Raiders and the Sea'—in the morning papers of England, Belgium and Holland, our landlady fairly beamed with pleasure and announced that she was preparing a *spécialité de la maison* for our evening meal. It was not only the fleeting blaze of notoriety which we had inadvertently brought to the Rue de l'Yser, but the arrival of a substantial cheque from my father which finally softened her heart and appealed to her commercial soul.

At last the wind dropped and the sea began to calm down; and, simultaneously, the crew of the Ostende life-boat set about the task of salvaging the *Imp*. Right from the beginning Captain Roetz, the Commandant of the Ostende pilotage, and the men who manned the life-boat had been quite marvellous. On the evening that we were wrecked they had searched the sea between Ostende and De Haan for several hours, not realizing that we were already ashore. And each subsequent day, around the time of high water, they had brought their boat out to try and rescue the *Imp*. But it was impossible while the gale continued to blow from the north. However, as soon as the wind died away the life-boat lorry drove along the beach at low tide and the men attached a strong hawser to the *Imp*'s bows and dragged her across the sand to the edge of the sea. Two of them remained aboard her—we were not allowed to accompany them—and when the tide started flooding the life-boat came in close and shot a rocket-line across on to her bows. Once this had been secured and she was just beginning to float, the life-boat towed her off the beach and into harbour; meanwhile the men who had remained aboard pumped and baled furiously to prevent her from sinking while under way. At last they brought the *Imp* safely into the Montgomery Dock, a dry-dock which the harbourmaster had said we might use while a firm of shipwrights patched up the hull and put the engine back into working order.

'I bet you'll wish she'd been swept out to sea by the time you get the bill for salvage!' one of the reporters had observed rather nastily.

Several other people confirmed his predictions, and warned me to expect a big salvage claim from the Ostende life-boat. In due course I receive their bill and opened it with some trepidation; but, much to my astonishment, it only came to 1280 Belgian francs (about £9), which was the amount required to cover the cost of fuel and ropes expended on the four-day salvage operation. For the rest of my life I shall carry a feeling of warmth and affection for Captain Roetz and the brave men of the Ostende life-boat, and also for the Belgian commandos who rescued us from the North Sea.

*   *   *   *   *

Winkle and I went home on the ferry as soon as the *Imp* was safely installed in the Montgomery Dock; but I returned to Ostende, alone, towards the end of August. By that time the temporary patching up of the hull had been completed and the engine repaired; but everywhere I looked there were particles of sand clinging to the boat, to remind me of our dreadful ordeal on the beach.

I set off next day in company with another small motor-boat which was also making for Dover. Hugging the coast as closely as we dared, we put into Nieuport, Gravelines and Calais, where I moored alongside the friendly tug, *Courageux*, once again. The crossing of the Dover Strait was made in a rough sea and poor visibility. I soon lost sight of the other boat, and the breaking waves on the Ridens de Calais caused the *Imp* to leak incessantly, so I divided my time between pumping out the bilges and attempting to keep the boat on course for Dover. I had not yet got over the effects of being shipwrecked—almost every night since then I had dreamt that we were swept out to sea in a gale and finally capsized—and the crossing seemed like a continuation of the familiar nightmare.

By the time the moon had risen and the great beam of the South Foreland Lighthouse had begun to probe the evening shadows, I had come to a very painful decision . . . this was going to be my last voyage across the Channel with the *Imp*. Never again would I be dependent upon an engine, as I was going to look for another boat and learn how to sail.

6. I LEARN TO SAIL

'Folkboat for sail. Built 1953 by Chippendale at Warsash. Won East Anglian Offshore Championship, 1954. Owner only selling because he wishes to build larger yacht.'

I jumped off the train at Burnham-on-Crouch, wondering if this was to be yet another abortive journey. Already I had spent over a year on the trail, writing and receiving scores of letters from boat-builders and yacht-brokers, and travelling to many harbours around the south and east coasts. It was hard to define exactly what I was looking for, but I knew, instinctively, that I had not yet found my ideal boat. But that last advertisement in *Yachting Monthly* held a certain promise—a hint of reluctance on the part of her present owner to part with her . . .

A bored-looking man in Newell Pettigrew's office told a boy to row me out to the Folkboat, *Martha McGilda*.

'That's 'er—the little blue one with the gold line round 'er top-strake,' announced my pilot when we were half way across the river. He raised a dripping oar and stabbed the air somewhere behind my left ear, at the same time sprinkling the back of my neck with ice-cold water. 'I'll drop you aboard so you can

I Learn to Sail

'ave a good decko on your own like, then come back for you later, O.K.?'

'O.K.,' I murmured dreamily. I had picked her out long before he pointed, and a small clear voice inside me was shouting 'That's your boat—you'll never find a better one than her!'

Martha McGilda combined all the finest qualities you could hope to find in a $2\frac{1}{2}$ ton sailing-boat, although it took me several years to appreciate this fact. She was beautiful to look at, fast and seaworthy, had perfect balance and she was light on the helm, so that a single-hander could sail her without becoming too exhausted; and, she had NO leaks in her clinker-built hull, something I found hard to believe until I had proved it in a very rough sea.

The boy rowed away in his dinghy and left me alone with my dream-boat. First I went into the cabin and sat down on one of the bunks; it certainly *was* different from the *Imp*—no standing headroom anywhere, and how strange the mast looked growing like a tree-trunk out of the middle of the cabin floor. A gently-arched half-bulkhead on either side led the eye forward to the long pointed fo'c'sle which was filled with an exciting assortment of unexplored treasures—coils of hemp and manilla rope, sail-bags, a small rubber dinghy, a pair of oars, a large tool-bag, a spare anchor, etcetera. The cabin décor was a medley of honey-gold varnish and sparkling white paintwork, with blue settee covers on either side. Everything was immaculate, both inside and out.

Presently I moved into the cockpit, and sitting on the stern-sheets I held the tiller with one hand and looked up in awe at the forest of rigging above me. Her tall mast seemed to touch the very clouds in the sky, and I pictured the great brown canvas mainsail filled with wind and the blue hull heeled far over, skimming across the shining green seas like some Arctic fulmar...

'What did you think of 'er?' asked the boy as he rowed me away from dreamland.

'Just perfect!' I sighed. 'But I wonder how her owner manages without an engine?'

'Mr Jordan is a proper sailor,' he snorted, fixing me with a scornful look. 'E don't need no lumps o' metal to 'andle 'is boat with; the wind's enough for 'im.'

I saw what he meant on my second visit to Burnham, when I was greeted by Noel Jordan, the great racing yachtsman, himself. A short stout man with an indomitable spirit, he combined an extraordinary mixture of idealism, optimism and courage with the ability to translate his dreams into the perfect living thing.

Martha McGilda was his second boat, built two years ago by the small firm of Chippendale at Warsash. Martha he told me, was the name of his mother-in-law, a lady of great determination and strength of character; and McGilda was an American slang word which meant sailing close to the wind. She was built from the exact lines of the original Scandinavian Folkboat, but Noel Jordan and Mr Chippendale between them had managed to weave some magic into her construction which made her poles apart from the common-or-garden Folkboat.

Noel had won every race for which he entered *Martha McGilda* during the 1954 sailing season and, encouraged by this success, he was now building a larger yacht at Prior's Yard in Burnham, with which he hoped to compete in a tougher class of R.O.R.C. racing. But one part of him—I suspected a very large part—could hardly bear the thought of selling little *Martha*. Right from the start I knew this could never be an ordinary business transaction in which one wrote out a cheque and received the goods in due course. I remembered Mr Cutts at West Mersea, and realized once again that a wooden boat should always be a living vibrant creature in the eyes of her owner, and not just a bundle of planks riveted together to form a boat. I paid £950 for *Martha McGilda*, and found that I had inherited a sacred trust as well as a hard reputation to live up to. Whenever I noticed a frayed rope end or a badly furled sail, the spirit of Noel Jordan bade me do something about it pretty quickly; and years later, his forceful lectures on the *right* way to do things on a sailing-boat invariably came back to me in moments of stress.

* * * * *

I Learn to Sail

A distant cousin of mine, Gillian Maude, bravely volunteered to accompany me on my first voyages in the new boat, and I soon discovered that she was the ideal sailing companion. A typical Piscean, with a tactful gentle nature, she was never dismayed by the uncertainty of our whereabouts or the roughness of the sea; and although she often suffered from seasickness, she would just be sick without any fuss, then start pumping out the bilges with a wide grin on her face two minutes later.

Extreme caution was the key-note of our first Channel crossing in *Martha McGilda*. Selecting a 'cruise in company' to Calais at Whitsuntide, we set off from Dover with about twenty other boats. It seemed rather choppy outside the harbour entrance, so I mentioned to Gillian that I was thinking of taking two reefs in the mainsail to be on the safe side—I had already practised this manoeuvre on the River Crouch with complete success. However, it was not so easy in the cross seas which meet off the South Foreland, and some half an hour later, when the last of the fleet was disappearing over the far horizon, we settled down on course for Calais.

There were so many new things to worry about such as our four-foot draught, involving intricate tidal calculations; the effect of leeway on our course, which could no longer be layed off from A to B with much conviction beforehand, especially when sailing close to the wind; and then there was that bogey I had never given a thought to before called compass error—but, at least, I now had a proper ship's compass for the first time in my life, which was a big improvement on the old prismatic one I had used on the *Imp*.

The wind was blowing a gentle Force 3 that day, and the crossing took us seven hours under double-reefed mainsail and working jib; but unfortunately it was not Calais, for which we were aiming, but Gravelines, which finally loomed up among the sand-dunes ahead of us. But Gillian was one of those happy people who appreciate any French port, no matter which one; and she exhibited an unexpected brilliance of repartee when we finally reached Calais the following day, and faced the storm of witticisms from our fellow yachtsmen.

Our next voyage that summer was the Prince of Wales Cup Race, a sixty-five mile course from Dover round the Dyck and

Varne Lightvessels, then across to Folkestone to avoid the foul tide on the return beat back to Dover. I felt driven to retrieve my reputation at the earliest opportunity, but this time I had taken the precaution of inviting Noel Jordan to accompany us on the race.

The morning shipping forecast gave fresh to strong north-easterly winds, but despite this gloomy outlook we sailed through the eastern entrance wearing our full mainsail and genoa. I was rather alarmed to see that there were only five boats gathered near the starting-line for this historic race, and *Martha* was certainly the smallest. *Vanity*, a 12-metre from Cowes with a crew of six, dwarfed the rest of the fleet; but even *Cedora*, an American 8-metre, and *José*, belonging to Doctor Melhuish from my home village of St Margaret's Bay, made our little Folkboat look like a dinghy.

'Haven't we got rather a lot of sail up?' I enquired tentatively of Noel, as the boat plunged up and down in the huge seas rebounding from the stone breakwaters.

'Oh, no! She can take a lot more than this breeze,' he chuckled happily, tucking the tiller firmly under one arm as he did up the last button on his oilskin.

Gillian, who cooked in a canteen in London during the week, had come well prepared with a freshly-roasted chicken which she had basted with a rich herb and wine sauce. I had brought a bottle of Traminer and another of Captain Morgan's rum to cheer us during the bleak hours ahead. Halfway between Dover and the Dyck Lightvessel I suggested a tot of rum to warm us up before lunch. We were all soaked in spite of our oilskins, and the north-east wind, which was blowing a good Force 6 by then, had a very keen edge to it.

'I never drink while I'm racing—plenty of time when we get back into harbour,' Noel declared firmly, with a hint of disapproval in his voice.

Gillian's teeth were chattering and she had already been sick twice, so I poured out a small measure which we shared rather furtively between us. Meanwhile, Noel remained wedded to the tiller, wearing an expression of total dedication and serenity. He kept a constant watch on the sails, the racing-flag, the waves and his adversaries, and he never seemed to suffer from cold,

I Learn to Sail

hunger, fear or sickness like the lesser mortals in his crew.

We rounded the Dyck Lightvessel after three hours, and immediately he announced that it was time to hoist the spinnaker.

'I'll steer,' I proposed brightly, not fancying a struggle with a mass of soaking cordage on the slippery foredeck, with those fearful white-crested waves breaking over the bows. Gillian and I both looked with longing towards the French coast which showed up very distinctly that afternoon: but a race, after all, is a race, and neither of us dared to voice such shameful thoughts.

Somewhere between the Dyck and the Varne the kicking-strap broke, and Noel said there was a chance of broaching to unless we sat quite still and kept her balance perfect. About the same time *Cedora*'s forestay snapped and she had to retire from the race; but *Vanity* and *José* were well ahead of us, and the only boat near enough to alleviate the total desolation of the scene was a Vertue called *Betsinda*.

During that awful run down Channel *Martha* exhibited a tendency to become airborne; but after the Varne she behaved more like a submarine. It was blowing N.E.7 by then, and even Noel admitted that a smaller headsail might be advantageous; and gallantly offered to attend to the sail changing himself. Every few seconds he disappeared from sight beneath some monstrous wave and I felt panic-stricken, wondering if we should ever see him again. But that heroic man always reappeared, smiling broadly—what did he find to smile about, I asked myself—and shaking himself like a dog with wet fur, he continued his hair-raising work on the foredeck.

Between Folkestone and Dover we were snugged down to a mere working jib and full mainsail, and sailing like a guided missile under the partial lee of the cliffs. The thought of Gillian's chicken, as yet unsampled—there had been no suitable opportunity to broach the subject of lunch—made us both more cheerful; Noel had never been anything else during the whole sixty-five-mile course.

It was blackest night and blowing great guns when we came surging through the eastern entrance of Dover Harbour on the crest of a mighty wave. It had taken us fourteen hours to complete the course. *José* won the race, on corrected time, and *Martha* came second.

'Not too bad for an inexperienced crew,' grinned Noel, as we devoured our chicken like ravenous wolves and washed it down with large tumblers of wine. 'But next time I expect you to come first!'

* * * * *

Inspired by our success in the Prince of Wales Cup Race, Gillian and I had planned a short voyage to Holland and back during our summer holidays. I finally decided on a compromise for *Martha McGilda*, and purchased a Seagull outboard engine with a long shaft. It clamped on to a special fitting on the starboard quarter when in use, and lived in a locker in the cockpit while we were sailing. 'I can always leave it at home if Noel comes again,' I told myself; 'and it may prove very useful if there's no wind at all.'

We crossed from Dover to Gravelines—intentionally, this time—but found that the wind was blowing straight down the narrow channel leading to the old walled town; however, this gave me a good excuse to try out the new engine. It started first pull and we motored proudly along the River Aa for some while, until we were abreast of the twin fishing ports of Grand and Petit Fort Philippe, when it suddenly petered out. By this time we had furled the sails and put everything away that might have been some use in an emergency. I pulled the starting-cord feverishly, tinkered with the carburettor and cursed the engine, but nothing would induce it to start; meanwhile the boat was drifting stern-first down the river, back towards the open sea.

'*Allô! Allô! Écoutez!*' bellowed a deep croaky voice from the shore. '*C'est defendu de naviguer à l'arrière entre les deux ports.*'

By this time I was hanging upside down like a bat over the starboard quarter, trying to dislodge a tattered chemise which had wrapped itself tightly round the propeller. 'Does the old idiot think we're navigating stern-first for pleasure?' I spluttered. 'Tell him to mind his own business!'

Gillian tactfully translated my reply as '*Notre moteur est en panne,*' and a local fisherman, appreciating our plight, asked if

I Learn to Sail

we had need of a man to assist us. Before we had time to reply, the chemise came free, almost taking me with it; then I pulled the starting-cord and the engine roared into life. We waved goodbye to our new shore acquaintances and motored on up the river to Gravelines.

The next two days were quite idyllic. A gentle breeze filled our sails and we sped northwards under the hot August sun; our feet trailed in the water on the leeward side of the boat and long lines of small black birds flew low over the sea on either hand. Gillian designed a pair of wide-brimmed sun-hats from the charts of the Dover Strait and the East Schelde Approaches, and our spirits were filled with the peace of the gentle fair-weather sailing noises which are so different from the thump and clatter of an internal combustion engine.

Beyond Ostende the wind died away—how different the beach below St Theresia looked from the last time I had seen it —so we motored eastwards for several hours, until the Seagull finally ran out of petrol.

'Nothing to worry about,' I assured Gillian, who was not exhibiting any signs of anxiety. 'We'll drop anchor and wait for the tide round the north coast of Walcheren Island.'

We anchored off Westkapelle Lighthouse, near the place where the Royal Marine Commandos made their desperate landings in 1944. We studied the beaches through our binoculars, then had a late lunch, after which we fell asleep. I woke when the flood tide set in, bringing small waves to chuckle and slap on the outside of *Martha's* clinker-built hull. How sad it would be, I reflected, to sail in a carvel-built boat and never hear the music of the waves as they serenaded the overlapping planks.

The sun was just setting when we hauled up the sails and got under way. A warm breeze came off the land, filled with the scent of wood-smoke, hay and cow-dung. *Martha* sailed fast along the north-west coast of Walcheren Island, but it was almost dark by the time we turned into the Roompot and away on our starboard quarter the little town of Domburg sprawled like a drowsy glow-worm under the royal-blue sky. Our bow-wave made a shining arc of phosphorescence, and quite close to us there were frogs croaking along the shore and lonely sea-birds calling to one another in the twilight.

At last we entered the Veregat, a narrow channel among the sandbanks marked by a meandering line of unlit buoys. The breeze blew from straight ahead so we were compelled to tack every two or three minutes which made it very difficult to steer a straight course down the middle of the channel. Gillian sat on the bows to keep a sharp lookout for buoys and sandbanks, while I steered and worked the sails. What with the sky being full of stars and the beauty of our emerald bow-wave, I felt quite bewitched and failed to hear her warning cry; a moment later *Martha* ran aground and sat there under the stars, with the sails slatting gently in the night breeze.

'I wonder where we are exactly,' murmured my patient cousin, voicing the thoughts which I had not liked to utter.

Presently we heard an old mellow clock chiming midnight, followed by a carillon of bells playing a hymn tune; and then I knew that we were perched on the edge of a famous sandbank called the Schotsman. But the tide was flooding fast, so we soon came afloat and started sailing again; and a few minutes later, like a dream come true, we could just make out the faint silhouette of the village of Veere.

We stole silently into the sleeping harbour with our mainsail casting giant shadows on the old Dutch houses along the fish quay. We moored alongside a botter, then Gillian and I put the boat to bed in whispers: I had the strange impression that *Martha* felt quite at home there already, and shared our delight in having made harbour under sail.

* * * * *

It was a year later before I attempted to sail *Martha* single-handed. That summer I had planned a voyage along the Normandy coast to Deauville, but Gillian was married in April and could not accompany me so I invited a neighbour, Barbara Wood, for the first few days; and I hoped to learn something of the art of single-handed sailing during the remaining two weeks.

Barbara left me at Le Tréport after we had made an exciting exploration of the River Canche estuary, watched Le Touquet transformed into a city of the Arabian Nights at sunrise, and had an unpleasant beat across the Somme Bay during which a gale warning was announced on the radio. She was a splendid

I Learn to Sail

helmswoman and a cheerful companion when the outlook was bleak, and I was very sorry to see her go.

There was a falling barometer and vile forecast to greet me next morning, but the wind did not seem too strong so I decided to sail along the coast to Dieppe as soon as the west-going tide set in. I managed to hoist all my sails before leaving harbour, an achievement of which I was rather proud as the outboard was more than likely to get swamped by the first big wave it met at the harbour entrance, unless it was stowed away inside its locker in good time. Assuming a confident old-sea-doggish expression, I tacked out of harbour waving to all the holiday-makers along the jetties at the end of each tack; sometimes it was the same ones twice running, as my progress was not remarkable for its speed.

A fresh wind was blowing from the north-west, and as soon as *Martha* had cleared the entrance I eased the sheets until we were on a close reach for Dieppe. The sailing was magnificent for the first few miles, and the boat flew across the waves like a seagull in sight of a shoal of fish. It was only thirteen and a half miles to Dieppe and we sailed the first ten miles in an hour and a half. I had just spotted the seaside resort of Belleville-sur-Mer on our port beam when the wind suddenly backed round to the west and freshened to Force 7, and the sun disappeared behind a dark bank of clouds. The waves soon started crashing into the cockpit, and my eyes stung so much with the salt water that I could hardly see. Remembering what had happened to the *Imp* between Blankenberghe and Ostende, I began to feel terribly frightened. I had already taken two reefs in the mainsail before leaving Le Tréport, in view of the morning forecast, so there was nothing else left to do apart from lowering the jib, which would not help me to reach Dieppe; and it was no use running back to Le Tréport as the entrance would only have about two feet of water in it by that time.

'I'll try ten minutes on the port tack and ten minutes on the starboard one; and thank goodness there's no engine to fuss about this time!' I told myself purposefully, for I had just caught a fleeting glimpse of the little seamen's church of Notre Dame de Bon Secours on the cliffs above Dieppe. That church was like a magnet, slowly drawing me towards the harbour entrance. I never took my eyes off it for one second, and I thought of all the seamen and fishermen who must have felt the first glimmer of hope, as I did then, when they were trying to make harbour in a storm.

Nevertheless, I *did* make harbour that evening, and there were no dramas on the rocky Pointe de Femme Grosse east of Dieppe.

* * * * *

The following day was Sunday, with the wind blowing even harder from the west. I felt quite relieved as there was no question of going to sea, and I looked forward to spending a quiet domestic day in harbour. I boiled some water with which to scrub the decks, but no sooner had I emerged from the cabin with my bucket and scrubber than three young men, who were making preparations for departure on a neighbouring fishing-boat, invited me to come with them for '*une petite promenade en mer*'.

'*Non, merci. J'ai le nettoyage à faire*,' I hastily replied, indicating my bucket of steaming water.

Their spokesman, a fair-skinned Norman whom I took to be the skipper of the *Soeur Thérèse*, declared that the cleaning could wait, and I must jump aboard '*toute de suite*'. I thought that I detected a note of challenge in his voice.

The quay above us was crowded with fishermen and their families taking a Sunday morning stroll, and all at once a sepulchral silence descended on the Avant Port—it seemed as if the whole of Dieppe was waiting to see what I would do. I had no desire to go to sea in that sort of weather or, for that matter, ever again after my passage from Le Tréport the previous day; but it was an embarrassing situation as the *Soeur Thérèse* had let go her lines and moved round to my port quarter, where her huge bows hung menacingly over my Red Ensign and her Diesel engine went choomph-a-choomph-a-choomph . . . like some great jungle beast breathing down my neck. On reflection there seemed to be no alternative, so I seized my oilskins and sea-boots, threw them aboard the fishing-boat and leapt after them. The audience on the quay above us began to cheer and shout '*Bonne chance!*' and '*Bon voyage!*' which did little to reassure me.

I Learn to Sail

The sea outside the harbour entrance was just as I had pictured it; a snow-capped mountain range—the Swiss Alps rather than the gentler undulations of the Pyrenees. But the *Soeur Thérèse* was a sturdy seine-net fishing-boat with a tremendous feeling of strength and endurance about her. After the initial shock of plunging into those mountainous seas, I was surprised to find how exciting and exhilarating it seemed—quite different from being alone in your own small boat with no one to laugh at you when a big wave breaks into the cockpit and soaks you to the skin!

Presently Bernard, the skipper, offered me the tiller—a vast baulk of timber, more like a telegraph pole—and dived into the cuddy for a bottle of red wine. His crew consisted of Robert, a boy with the jaunty appearance of a Mid-Western cow-boy, and Alexandre, whose lively dark brown eyes and expressive gestures could only belong to a true Frenchman.

Bernard opened the bottle of wine and we four shared it between us, with the heaving thundering waves breaking over the bows and the air filled with the cries of seagulls and the wild sea-wind, which tore at our hair and blew the salt spray into our eyes. Alexandre explained to me that they went out fishing for six nights of the week, but never on Sundays; that was the day when they slept at home and took the holiday-makers out for *'promenades en mer'* in fine weather.

'Like today?' I asked with interest.

'*Exactement*,' he replied, with the grin of a mischievous monkey. 'Just now we have come to take a *'coup d'oeil'* at the sea to assure ourselves that it is suitable for the afternoon *'voyageurs'*!

On our way back into harbour Bernard pointed out the fishermen's quarter of Le Pollet, nestling on the cliffs below the little church of Notre Dame de Bon Secours. They had all been born and bred there, he told me, and they had a special way of pronouncing certain words of which they were very proud; for instance, anyone who referred to *'la mer'* as *'la mè'* would instantly be recognized as a true son of Le Pollet.

Back in the Avant Port an enormous woman with a mass of jet black hair piled high on top of her head, and more than a hint of a black moustache, was enticing the tourists in stentorian tones to take *'une petite promenade en mer'*.

'We call her "*la Vache Noire*",' Robert informed me as we came alongside the steps.

She changed her patter as soon as she noticed me aboard the *Soeur Thérèse*, and announced that '*la petite Anglaise*' had sailed the Atlantic single-handed, and without doubt the brave gentlemen of France would desire to prove their valour by escorting this little foreigner, who had no fear of the sea!

I stayed aboard the *Soeur Thérèse* all afternoon, and we took out boatload after boatload of unsuspecting Parisians, some of whom had never set eyes on the sea before. They sent up prayers to their favourite saints as we approached the harbour entrance, then some of them screamed with terror while others were violently seasick. Once we were well clear of the entrance the three fishermen usually left me to steer, advanced the throttle to full ahead and dived below into the cuddy. Presently they would reappear, all wearing life-jackets, which invariably caused great consternation among the female passengers.

'Are you never afraid of the sea?' I asked Alexandre, wondering at their strange sense of humour.

'No, never' he replied. 'I have St Thérèse to guard me'—he showed me a silver medallion of the saint which he wore on a chain round his neck—'*et enfin*, the sea is our life, *n'est-ce pas?*' He shrugged his shoulders and spread out his hands in a gesture which explained everything.

We returned from our last trip about six o'clock, and I was invited to join the fishermen and their families for drinks in a large bar called *Au Roi de la Bière*. It seemed to me that half the inhabitants of Le Pollet were there that evening, and prominent among them was *la Vache Noire* who regaled the company with a vivid account of her young days at sea. I felt extraordinarily proud and delighted to be included in their Sunday evening family party. It soon transpired that each of the three boys had some relative working in another port along the coast of Normandy—for instance, the keeper of the signal station at Le Tréport was Bernard's uncle; the captain of a dredger in Le Havre was Alexandre's father and the patronne of a café in St Valery-en-Caux was Robert's sister-in-law. When I left Dieppe and sailed on down the coast, everywhere I went their

I Learn to Sail

relatives would suddenly appear and make me welcome in their own harbours.

That summer I visited St Valery-en-Caux, Fécamp, Le Havre, Honfleur and Deauville. The winds were moderate and the sun shone every day, and gradually I learnt how to handle the boat by myself; but the best thing of all was the warm happy feeling of sailing among friends.

I stopped in Dieppe for a few hours on the way home, but it was mid-week and there was no sign of the *Soeur Thérèse* in the Avant Port. I had planned to make an early start next morning and at 6 a.m., when I crawled on deck still half asleep, I found a giant sole wrapped in the latest edition of *La Voix du Nord*, lodged in a corner of the cockpit. The *Soeur Thérèse* was moored nearby, rocking gently in the wash of a passing tug, but her crew had all gone home to sleep.

There was a thick white fog that morning as I stole out to sea in the silent dawn. Even the lighthouse on the harbour entrance looked like some ghostly sentinel, and as soon as I had swung *Martha* round on to a north-easterly course, there was nothing else to see. I felt lonely and sad in that empty white world, and the Red Ensign drooped from the flagstaff in sympathy with my mood. After twenty minutes or so I glanced back over my right shoulder, and there was Notre Dame de Bon Secours floating in a sea of pale pink clouds, high above the port of Dieppe which remained shrouded in the mist.

* * * * *

There was no wind at all for the last lap of my voyage from Boulogne to Dover. I ran the Seagull for several hours and could already make out the silhouette of Dover Castle some miles ahead, when an extraordinary mishap took place. I had left the mainsail up with the boom right out, hoping to catch an occasional breath of wind from astern; and suddenly the mainsheet dipped into the sea, then took a lightning turn round the petrol tank on the outboard engine and pulled taut before I could reach it; a moment later the tank had been wrenched right off the engine and disappeared with a loud plop into the depths of the sea!

An uncanny silence then ensued, with no engine and no wind

—just *Martha* and I bobbing up and down in the gentle swell. What on earth should I do now, I asked myself rather helplessly; then it came to me in a flash. I hauled the tiny rubber dinghy out of its bag in the fo'c'sle, spent a hectic half hour pumping it up with a pair of ancient bellows, then lowered myself gingerly into the middle of it with a strong line round my waist which was attached to *Martha*'s samson-post at the other end; and, finally, I began to row. It was very hard work towing my boat back home with a rubber dinghy, which is not easy to row effectively, even on a duck-pond. But there was nothing else to be done so I rowed and rowed and rowed, and the towing-line bit into my skin as *Martha* swerved from one side to the other because there was no one to steady her helm.

I was beginning to feel worn out and rather worried, as it was almost dusk and I had not been able to light the navigation lamps; also the south-going tide was setting in and would soon be flowing strongly across the harbour entrance. Then one of those miracles happened which seemed specially reserved for landlubbers at large on the open sea—a heavensent breeze sprang up from the west. I clambered hastily back into *Martha*'s cockpit, transferred the tow-rope from my waist to the bows of the dinghy, then hauled in the sheets and *Martha* and I, towing the dinghy astern, sailed happily across the twilight seas to Dover.

7. SAILING TO RUSSIA

I. THE NORTH SEA

'Why don't you sail across the Atlantic or round the world, instead of setting off on this crazy trip to Russia?' suggested the young reporter from the *Southern Evening Echo*. 'I mean, if you did something really sensational, or got yourself rammed by a whale and shipwrecked, I could write a splendid story about you!'

'I'm sorry to disappoint you,' I laughed, 'but I should be scared stiff out in the middle of the Atlantic. Besides I've always wanted to sail across the Baltic, and Russia happens to be at the other end of it. Most professional seamen think that it's more dangerous to navigate in unfamiliar coastal waters than to cross an ocean, you know; think of all the hair-raising pilotage I shall have to do!'

'I dare say; but it sounds quite ordinary in print,' he sighed. 'Tell me, at least, what it is that attracts you about single-handed sailing? You don't strike me as being the solitary type at all!'

I often asked myself the same question but there was no ready answer, for the role of a seafaring female is seldom an easy one. Most women go sailing to accompany their husbands or boyfriends, and not because they really enjoy being at sea in the first place; and in many cases their subsequent experiences are not encouraging. I mean who would really want to cook several meals a day for five or six hungry men in a space which is hardly big enough to house a couple of guinea-pigs? And that tiny space inclined at an angle of 45°, but not a constant angle; for no sooner have you wedged yourself and your pans into positions of comparative security, than your tiny world tips 45° over the other way, leaving a trail of disaster in its wake. Supposing at that precise moment the man of your choice pushes open the main hatch, perceives a delta of Irish stew flanked by rivulets of brown gravy in the middle of his latest chart of the English Channel, and addresses you in terms which lack some of their customary warmth and affection, who could blame you for deciding to stay at home in future?

Apart from the *Arabella* episode, I had been fortunate enough to possess my own boat for some years, to steer her all day and all night if there was no one else aboard, and to do all the really interesting things like navigation and boat-handling in difficult conditions and keep the household chores strictly in the background, reserved for intervals when there was nothing better to do.

But it was not long after I started single-handed sailing that I became aware of the severity of public opinion about a woman afloat on her own. It was all right, apparently, if you crossed the Atlantic or sailed round the world on a tea-tray, with plenty of Press coverage; then, at least, all the land women knew that you were out of harm's way for x number of months. But what they quite definitely did *not* approve of was a floating female at large off the North European seaboard, within easy reach of a number of popular harbours.

From my own point of view I found single-handed sailing a mixed pleasure. It was made up of complete peace and happiness or gibbering fright and wet freezing misery out at sea, followed by unpredictable encounters on reaching harbour. I was seldom left alone for long, which could be very trying after a hard wet day when all I wanted was a tin of baked beans and the warm interior of my sleeping-bag. The approaches varied from one harbour to the next: on Monday it might be a frigid questionnaire about my nautical ability from a very pusserlooking yachtsman who had remembered to lower his ensign on the dot of sunset; and on Tuesday an immediate invitation to a few snifters before a late supper aboard a neighbouring yacht whose owner was in the middle of changing his crew, the old ones having just departed and the new ones not yet arrived; on Wednesday a prolonged visit from the local customs and police, scenting the possibilities of some hideous crime owing to the absence of any visible male in charge; and on Thursday a lightning abduction by an intensely hospitable and dominating shore couple who rushed me back home, some good few miles inland, in a very sick-making limousine and then popped me straight into a scalding hot bath!

However, half the charm of going to sea is not knowing what the next day has in store. And I set sail on my two thousand mile voyage to the eastern end of the Baltic feeling like Odysseus may have felt when he embarked on his voyage back to Ithaca.

* * * * *

There is no doubt that the success or failure of most voyages depends largely on the extent of the forethought and preparations which have taken place before the ship leaves harbour. Never having attempted a voyage of that magnitude before, I started making plans and detailed lists nearly a year beforehand. They came under four headings—the boat, stores, crew and return voyage.

Martha was really no problem as I sailed her back to Mr Chippendale who had built her in 1953, and whose small yard was tucked away up Fareham Creek; and she spent all the winter there having a thorough overhaul of her hull, spars and rigging. He placed her on the quay outside his office, and built a little house around her to protect her from the winter gales; and I spent many happy hours in there, scraping, sand-papering and repainting the inside of her hull, and dreaming about the long voyage we would make together in a few months' time.

The stores, apart from the ordinary summer's cruising gear, included engine spares, tools, a sail-mending bag, pilotage books and tidal atlases, eight dictionaries and courtesy flags—the French, Belgian, Dutch, German, Danish, Swedish, Finnish and Russian—extra life-saving and fire-fighting equipment, blocks, shackles, cooker spares, paint and varnish, a great deal of tinned food and jars of coffee and jam, a large first aid box, new ropes of various sizes, Lux soap-flakes and plenty of clothes'-pegs, extra warm jerseys and trousers for the Finnish autumn (which starts about the end of August), films, books, sketching materials and scores of charts.

The question of crew was the hardest one of all to solve. I wanted to make the whole voyage single-handed for a number of reasons but my mother, having lost my father a year or so previously and living on her own for much of the time, was filled with gloomy forebodings at the thought of me sailing alone in strange waters for three or four months. In the end we reached a compromise, and I invited Gillian for the first weekend which was all that she could manage, and Barbara Wood for various parts of the voyage which fitted in with her own family arrangements and children's school holidays. And, finally, I agreed to leave *Martha* in Holland or Germany and come home for a short interval during the month of June.

Our return passage at the end of the summer—for Barbara, *Martha* and myself—was booked on a timber-carrying freighter trading between London and Helsinki, and Mr Chippendale made a special cradle for *Martha* which was shipped out to Finland in September.

* * * * *

Launching day was March 26th, and *Martha* slid out of her winter quarters like a butterfly emerging from its chrysalis. She stood on the quay in her glistening new coats of sky-blue paint, oblivious of the raindrops pattering down on her cabin-top, of the group of people collected in front of her, discussing her, praising her and even daring to touch her. At last the crane plucked her out of the cradle and swung her outwards, over the still grey waters of Fareham Creek. There was a breathless hush, and I was acutely aware of every trivial detail around me; a flight of gulls heading towards Portsmouth Harbour; a raindrop settling on a man's moustache; the smell of wet timber coming from the stack behind the shed. For one moment in eternity *Martha* became the supreme focus of all existence, poised there in all her glory ... the moment passed, and she was lowered briskly into the waiting sea.

Some twelve hours later I lay in my bunk listening to the young flood creeping up round my boat. First the mud of Fareham Creek sighed and sucked and gurgled, then the water started its gentle lapping against the hull. The little voices which lure us out to sea each springtime had begun to call again, and I was glad that the long winter was over.

I made a fast single-handed passage from Fareham to Rye, with a strong south-west wind on the quarter most of the way; in fact it was so fast that I was quite unable to come to a halt inside Rye Harbour, which I had planned as my first night's resting-place.

There can be certain complications about the arrival under sail in a small harbour on your own. If you remove some of the canvas too soon, you may find yourself caught in stays right in the neck of the entrance, with a strong current sweeping you back out or a mammoth concrete pier-head bearing down on you at alarming speed. On the other hand, if you sail in rather magnificently with everything up you possess, there may not be enough room to turn up into the wind and get something down before making your arrival felt. On that occasion I had chosen the latter approach, but each time I selected my quarry to come alongside and bore down upon her under a press of canvas, I found it quite impossible to leave the tiller for long enough to sprint up for'ard and lower the mainsail. It was blowing Force 7 that evening, and Rye Harbour is situated on a narrow river with a fierce tide rushing along it; four times I sped up and down that congested ribbon of water with Jack Doust, the harbour-master, bawling instructions at me whenever I flashed by, and some of the local fishermen leaping from one moored boat to another armed with huge fenders, their faces furrowed with anxiety. My voyage to Russia might have come to an untimely end had not Jack taken a flying leap from his dinghy during my fourth circuit, and landed neatly on *Martha*'s stern. After that it was child's play for me to lower the sails while he steered the boat and held her head to wind.

The following day I sailed round to Dover in a seemly manner, and attached *Martha* to a mooring-buoy in the outer harbour where she remained for the next few weeks while I made my final preparations.

Several months after sending in an application for a visa to sail in Russian waters, I received a terse reply from the Russian Embassy saying *Niet*; one definitely was *not* permitted to sail in the eastern end of the Baltic. This merely served as a challenge, and the following day I bought a Russian courtesy flag.

* * * * *

Gillian and I set sail for France on May 16th. It was the Royal Cinque Ports Yacht Club's annual race from Dover to Calais, and seemed an appropriate day on which to start my voyage. I was very thankful to have her with me that week-end, as many of the people I was most fond of, together with my dog, Pierrot, were clustered round the signal station at the end of the Eastern Arm to wave me goodbye. As we sailed through the harbour entrance I felt more like crying my eyes out than taking part in a race.

We sailed to France by the feel of the wind on our faces that day, as the visibility was very poor and the compass needle swung wildly to and fro through an arc of 60°, which seemed a bad omen at the start of my voyage. It was not until several days later that I traced the cause of this behaviour to a tin of *foie gras*, a parting gift from one of my friends, which I had hastily pushed into the stern locker only a few inches away from the compass. (For those who are unconversant with the mysteries of compass deviation, it was the tin and not the foie gras which excited the needle!)

Four hours later we were astonished to see Calais harbour entrance looming out of the mist ahead of us; but even more astonished when we crossed the finishing line and they told us that we had won the race! Later that evening fifteen sailing-boat crews celebrated together in the yacht club, and Gillian and I were the conquering heroines. I felt triumphant and the long voyage ahead of me presented no problems; it was bound to be a success after such a magnificent start.

Gillian and most of the others returned to England on Sunday afternoon, and a strong east wind began to howl in my rigging; and, at last, there was plenty of time to reflect on the sober facts.

I had lost all the exultation of a conquering heroine by then, and realized that I was very lonely and rather frightened; why, in the name of common-sense, had I made those boastful announcements to everyone at home about intending to sail to Russia!

The east wind continued to blow lustily for the next nine days, and I made mouselike sallies out to sea from time to time, creeping very slowly north-eastwards along the French and Belgian coasts. I hated everything to do with sailing-boats that week, and thought with deep nostalgia of the dear old *Imp*. It had been so simple to lower the mast on a boat like that, and then one could enter the canal system and keep moving peacefully towards one's objective for days on end; but with a boat which had a deep keel and tall fixed mast there was no alternative but to beat out to sea and struggle against those hateful North Sea combers.

At one stage between Dunkerque and Nieuport the wind suddenly brisked up to Force 7, so I hove to and reefed the mainsail very badly owing to the heavy pitching motion in the shallow seas. As a result, the after end of the boom was much lower than the for'ard end by the time I had finished, but somehow I managed to tack upwind until I reached Nieuport. Sailing along the narrow channel leading to the fishing harbour, the boom suddenly swung across and hit me a resounding blow on the side of the head, knocking me unconscious, after which I collapsed in a crumpled heap on the floor of the cockpit! When I came to, *Martha* had run aground on a neighbouring mudbank and a woman pushing a perambulator along the tow-path was gaping at me with a look of astonishment in her eyes. Luckily the tide was still flooding so *Martha* soon came unstuck, and we sailed on up the river to Nieuport town.

Next morning I was sitting on the cabin-top securing the slides to the foot of the mainsail with some strong new lashings when a Belgian yachtsman, working on an old fishing-boat alongside *Martha*, asked where I was bound for.

'Finland,' I replied—Russia, I had discovered, always made people look at one in a funny way.

'*Tiens! tiens! C'est assez loin ça, n'est-ce pas?*' he shook his head vigorously several times, and gave me a searching look with his violet-blue eyes. He was a man of about thirty-five, dressed rather stylishly for *le sport nautique*, and his remark struck me as being sympathetic and intelligent, judging by my rate of progress during the past few days; then I thought of my old school atlas at home, on which the distance from Dover all the way to Leningrad was only the length of my middle finger laid across the map!

An hour or so later I had just hauled up the mainsail and was casting off the mooring lines when my Belgian friend, who had been home for lunch, leapt aboard his boat and handed me a formal visiting-card bearing the legend, 'Paul Luyten of 20, Avenue Albert I, Nieuport.'

'You will send me a little word to announce your safe arrival in Finland, if you please?' he demanded anxiously, arresting my departure with a strong hand gripping my shrouds.

'Yes, with pleasure!' I laughed, wondering if I should ever reach Holland, let alone Finland. But I sailed away down the river feeling less tragic, and the idea of sending Paul Luyten a postcard from my first port in Finland became a dreamlike zenith to strive towards in the months ahead.

* * * * *

I wasted three more days in Ostende waiting for an easterly gale to blow itself out. Mind you, there were plenty of other sea-mice like me, glued to their radios whenever the shipping forecasts were due, busily sketching in tight bunches of isobars on their home-made weather maps, and constantly paying furtive visits to the sea front to cast an anxious eye over the angry waves. 'Low pressure diarrhoea' one yachtsman called it, and I began to see what he meant by the third day.

On the fourth morning I finally set sail for Holland. It was a real North Sea day, full of the joy of living; the sun shone brilliantly out of a cloudless apple-green sky and the sea was a dirty olive colour, sprinkled with dazzling white horses; and, miraculously, the wind had dropped to a mere Force 4. I lashed the tiller for a while and lay on my back in the cockpit, watching the top of the mast gyrating against the brilliant sky and the gentle arc of the red canvas mainsail curving up into the boundless heavens. There were small Flemish gulls crying raucously to each other in mid-air and everything smelt of seaweed and salt water. All the bad days were swept aside in a flash, and there was no longer any question of failure or success; I was only aware of the wonder of being alive in the middle of all that glory.

I reached Flushing in the afternoon, and motored through the Middelburg Canal to Veere. Sitting by the west window in the Campveerse Toren, chatting with Henk and watching the sun go down behind the sandbanks in the Veregat, was a mistake. The magic spell which drew me back to Veere year after year was hard at work that evening, and I felt all my incentive to sail to Russia crumbling away and being replaced by a strong desire to stay where I was and do nothing more ambitious than a little mild exploring among the Dutch islands ... then I remembered Paul Luyten and the postcard; and for the next ten days I sped north-eastwards across Holland at a remarkable speed.

I have to admit that this was not entirely my own doing. After two days of hard sailing against a strong and squally north wind, I reached the Voorne Canal, just south of Rotterdam, in rather poor condition. I was wet, tired and having trouble with my Seagull—this rarely happened, as it was one of the most splendid and reliable small engines I have ever possessed; but that particular week it was definitely off-colour and, eventually, ground to a halt near the entrance to the busy locks at Hellevoetsluis. It was then that an Englishman travelling in the same direction suddenly came to my rescue; seeing a helpless female spinning round and round in a whirlpool caused by the thrust of the propellers of some gigantic barges, with a flick of his wrist he lassoed the samson-post on *Martha*'s bows and calmly towed me into the lock.

Colonel Stevens was a retired army officer making a single-handed voyage from the Isle of Wight to Sweden in his five-ton sloop, *Query*. A man of strong character and iron determination, tempered by a streak of old-fashioned chivalry, his voyages were carefully planned and took on something of the nature of a military campaign. Having rescued me from impending disaster, the kind-hearted Colonel then offered to tow *Martha* across Central Holland, an offer which was hard to refuse. Thus we travelled in company through the mighty port of Rotterdam, with hordes of tugs and barges pounding along behind us and freighters the size of sky-scrapers manoeuvring across our course; then up the River Ijssel to Gouda, and from there through Alphen and Haarlem to the North Sea Canal, and finally into Amsterdam; by that time we were scarcely on speaking terms.

The trouble may have been that I was swayed by the basest motives in accepting his offer of a tow; I knew perfectly well that I should be able to advance much more rapidly under tow from a powerful inboard engine, than I could ever hope to do with my own little Seagull battling away on the starboard quarter. But I hated the idea of being towed and imagined that all the world must think I had broken down or was incapable of managing my own boat; this hurt my pride and made me very bad-tempered. Colonel Stevens, for his part, was probably appalled by my ungrateful behaviour when he was expending valuable time and horse-power on my behalf; but his chivalrous nature forbade him to cast me adrift as he had the lowest possible estimation of my nautical expertise!

On the third day we emerged into the Zuyder Zee and both boats were able to hoist their sails for a change, which conduced a marked improvement in the atmosphere. We visited the charming old towns of Hoorn and Enkhuizen, then sailed on in company across the Zuyder Zee to Lemmer. There was a strong west wind blowing that day, with a hollow breaking sea rolling up on the quarter. Nearing the Friesland shore, I noticed that *Query* seemed a longish way farther south, and suddenly I saw a blinding flash of light erupt from her cockpit.

'I'd better gybe over that way and see if the poor man has had some awful accident?' I thought to myself. 'Perhaps I can be of some assistance.'

By the time I got within hailing distance it was perfectly clear that there was nothing wrong with *Query* or her owner, apart from a singed index finger and a filthy temper! It appeared that I had been steering about 10° off course and my Dutch chart had the depths marked in decimeters, not fathoms, a detail I had failed to grasp as I headed cheerfully towards a shoal with one foot of water over it. So Colonel Stevens let off a distress flare to warn me, and it had burnt his finger and, worse still, all his previous convictions about damnfool women in charge of boats had now been confirmed!

The province of Friesland was so beautiful that it had a soothing effect on our frayed nerves. It is a region of ancient farmhouses, piebald cattle and majestic cart-horses which graze in lonely splendour under the gigantic dome of the sky. The canal banks were lined with yellow irises and clumps of coarse grass, the haunt of innumerable ducks and reed-warblers; and there was something indescribably earthy and intoxicating about the smell of that Friesian landscape. During our three-day voyage across the shining meres and along the shallow canals where we often ran aground, it was an everyday occurrence to see a cart-horse on a small flat barge, being ferried along the canal to some fresh pasture or place of toil.

On the third evening we reached the Lauwerzee, a U-shaped indentation in the Dutch coastline with the island of Schiermonnikoog silhouetted against the northern sky. It was a wild and forlorn place like I imagined some remote corner of the moon might be. We sailed across a troubled yellowish sea, following a tortuous channel marked by slender perches and occasional buoys. All around us were miles and miles of sandbanks revealed by the ebbing tide, and away in the northern distance Schiermonnikoog Lighthouse loomed up like some gaunt sentinel, guarding the shores of Holland from the thundering North Sea breakers. It was my first thrilling glimpse of the Friesian Islands, those desolate blobs of sand strung out like a necklace across the southern fringe of German Bight.

We reached the lock at Zoutkamp that evening, and *Query* towed *Martha* for the last time along a broad winding canal until we came to the city of Groningen. I was running behind schedule as so often happens on a boat; already it was June and, remembering my promise to return home for two or three weeks, I made arrangements to leave *Martha* in the yacht harbour there and flew back to England the following day.

* * * * *

I returned to Groningen with Barbara Wood some three weeks later and found, to my astonishment, that *Martha* had freshly painted decks and an awning over her cockpit to shield it from the hot sunshine. I shall always remember the kindness of the yachtsmen of Groningen, who lavished such care and attention on the boat during my absence.

We sailed along the busy Ems Canal to Delfzijl, then out into the River Ems on a lovely summer's day. We had two large-scale German charts and a much-thumbed copy of *The Riddle of the Sands*, and we followed the winding channel through the Bants Balje and then over the watershed south-west of Norddeich, crossing the track of Davies and Carruthers in their dinghy when they set off from Norderney in a thick fog to pay a secret visit to Dollmann's depot on Memmert. The sun set gloriously behind the Memmert Beacon, and it was very peaceful out there among the sandbanks with only a few small seabirds twittering and an occasional seal barking discreetly under the stars.

Because it was fine weather and I had no local knowledge, I took some foolish risks during the next few days which nearly put a premature end to our voyage. Leaving Norderney next morning, we tacked into a brisk east wind across the watershed behind the island, then darted out to sea through the Wichter Ee, a little used gap between Norderney and Baltrum. No sooner had we gained the open sea than the barometer started to fall and cirrus clouds came racing in from the west.

'Perhaps we'd better pop back in through the next gap,' I told Barbara, glancing at the sky without enthusiasm.

Neither of us had bothered to read the pilotage book at that stage, so we sailed boldly in through the Ackumer Ee, then dropped anchor between the two islands to wait for enough water to enter the little drying-out harbour at Langeoog. As soon as the boat had settled I glanced at the chart and noticed a spot marked '*Ankern verboten*' off the eastern end of Baltrum; so I took a pull at our anchor chain and it absolutely refused to budge. Presently two German boys swam out from the beach to offer their assistance and assure us that we had most certainly hooked the submarine cable which runs between the two islands! We all heaved and hauled and jumped around on the foredeck, and the boys dived under the boat several times, but they could not shift the anchor as the tide was too strong and the water too cold to stay below for long.

Sailing to Russia

Later on we held a conference in the cockpit, with a few swigs of whisky to warm up our helpers. Everyone agreed that the C.Q.R.—our only reliable anchor—was as good as lost; and I began to feel very downcast. Noticing this, one of the boys who was a student from the little town of Norden, told me that he was building a boat in his garden at home but it would not be finished for another year, and as he owned a big strong anchor he would lend it to me with great pleasure and I could return it to him sometime the following winter. Barbara and I were very touched by this marvellous offer to a pair of foreigners and total strangers, who might never be heard of again; but we were determined to make one last effort to free the anchor at slack water, before cutting the chain.

At 7 p.m. a fresh squally wind was blowing and we hoisted both sails and drove *Martha* ahead at full speed, first on one tack then on the other, with the boys hauling on the anchor chain with all their might. Suddenly they collapsed in a heap on the foredeck and the boat leapt forward like a bird released from its cage: by some miracle we had sailed the fluke of the anchor out from under the cable, and there was much rejoicing as we hauled it safely back on board. After saying goodbye to our splendid new friends, we sailed happily across to Langeoog Harbour.

A northerly gale was blowing next morning so we decided to stay put until the weather improved. I loved Langeoog with its lonely windswept beaches and low hills covered in gorse and heather. There were no cars on the island, but a miniature train ran between the harbour and the small red-roofed town; and there were also some horse-drawn buggies which came to fetch passengers arriving on the daily ferry from Norddeich.

We made friends with the young German couple on a sailing-boat called *Klabauter*, moored alongside us; and Klaus, her red-headed owner, spent most of the afternoon popping in and out of his for'ard hatch like a jack-in-a-box, clutching a wide variety of different bottles and saying to us in his very precise English; 'I wish you now to prove this bottle!'

Barbara can hold her own with distinction in any contest of that nature, and after the seventh bottle Klaus confided to us that, generally speaking, he found the English a race who were totally devoid of any sense of humour, but he could assure us, from the heart, that we were delightful exceptions to the rule!

The wind had dropped to a fresh north-westerly breeze next morning, so we said goodbye to Klaus and his family and sailed away eastwards along an insignificant gully called, by some freak of maritime nomenclature, the Neuharlingersieler Wattfahrwasser. Presently the sandbanks began to uncover; tones of mauve and zircon-blue as the wet sand emerged from the shallow sea, then the amber glints which turned to gold as the sun beat down upon the banks. On the far horizon a shrimp fisherman stood out in stark relief, a sombre black outline with his great square nets submerged beneath the water.

After an hour or so we drew away from the mainland and, sailing closer to the wind, felt our way cautiously along a tortuous channel marked by rather dubious perches. Blinding sheets of spray flew across the boat from time to time; I dabbed at my glasses with a damp piece of cotton-waste and peered ahead anxiously until I saw a large striped buoy with a north-pointing triangle as a top-mark, bouncing up and down in the olive-coloured sea. This, I knew, was the first guardian of the difficult exit between Langeoog and the next island.

As we approached the gap, Barbara unwisely thumbed through the North Sea Pilot and read out the following extract —'Otzumer Balje is the passage between Langeoog and Spiekeroog. The frequent changes in the channel often render its marking useless, as some time must elapse before the buoys can be moved to correspond with the alterations. The passage is, however, used by boats with local knowledge, navigating by sight of the breakers.'

The breakers were there all right, on three sides of us, and when we were half way though the gap the wind suddenly died and, simultaneously, the metal fitting which connects the boom to the mast split in two and the boom began to swing wildly about from one side to the other. In a matter of seconds *Martha* had been transformed into a helpless boat without sail-power, drifting rapidly towards a fearsome sandbank called the Süder Riff where we should be smashed to pulp by those enormous thundering breakers. There was no time to sit down and think things out—Barbara dived head-first into the fo'c'sle and grabbed the C.Q.R., and I hauled twenty-five fathoms of rope and chain out of the stern locker and shackled it on to the anchor with trembling fingers. A stern voice—perhaps Noel Jordan's—admonished me while I worked; 'Always have your anchor ready on deck in the future; you should *know* that by now, after all the time you've spent at sea!'

Martha was right on the edge of that sailor's graveyard when the anchor gripped the sea-bed and, miraculously, it held. I crawled up for'ard and put a temporary lashing round the boom, then prised our wonderful Seagull from its locker and clamped it on to the starboard quarter. It started immediately despite the cascades of water pouring all over the boat. Barbara, attached to the mast by a few turns of the main halyard, hauled in the anchor while I steered and worked the engine controls. As soon as the anchor had broken free we headed into the least vicious-looking jumble of breakers, as the buoyed channel seemed to have disappeared from sight.

By the time we had gained the open sea I felt certain that we had been saved by some miracle which had little to do with our own puny efforts at self-preservation. Supposing the anchor had dragged, or we had lost it off Baltrum, or the engine refused to start, or one of us had been swept overboard ... there were so many fearful contingencies, and both of us felt a marvellous sensation of wonder and delight in our everyday surroundings, now that the horror of the Otzumer Balje lay some distance away on the starboard beam.

I mended the fitting which joins the boom to the mast, then we sailed slowly and peacefully across the wide estuaries of the Jade and Weser until we came to the Elbe. The night was full of stars and flashing and occulting lights, and with the dawn came a fresh breeze from the south-east to speed us past the Refuge Beacon on the Scharhörn Riff. How dark and forbidding it looked in the grey half-light, but already we had passed Elbe No. 1 Lightvessel, and the broad fairway of the river lay ahead. Presently the tide turned and we joined the pageant of shipping sweeping towards the land on the flood. We sailed past the busy port of Cuxhaven, and at last, some thirty hours after leaving Langeoog, *Martha* entered the locks at Brunsbüttel at the southern end of the Kiel Canal.

II. THE BALTIC

I came round very slowly, out of a deep dreamless sleep. I did not want to wake up, or watch the sunbeams playing on the deckhead, or face any fresh problems . . . but there was someone knocking insistently on the cabin-top. At last I sat up in my bunk and saw an immensely fat German lady peering in through the cabin door.

'*Guten morgen!*' she greeted me, baring a set of gleaming false teeth. 'I hope you haf gut slept?'

I had not yet reached the stage where I was prepared to admit to having slept well, but she was unaware of this and soon made the purpose of her visit known.

'I haf a daughter, married and living in America,' she informed me nostalgically; 'and she has exactly your dimensions! For this reason it vill gif me great pleasure to arrange a tau for you, through our great Nord-Ostsee Kanal.'

I thanked her very much for her kindness, but as soon as she was out of earshot Barbara murmured pensively, 'I wonder if the daughter in America has the same dimensions as her mother?'

At four o'clock next morning we set off at a speed of eight knots along the Kiel Canal, behind the German coaster, *Fortuna*; and some ten hours later we emerged into the Baltic Sea, having paid the skipper of the coaster 20 marks and moved briskly across sixty miles of Schleswig Holstein.

The next few days were something of an anti-climax. The Baltic seemed dull and uninspiring after the North Sea, and Sønderborg, our first Danish port, left a disagreeable impression as we were moored downwind of a slaughterhouse for three dreadful days during a gale.

I had always pictured the Baltic as a huge lake—calm, peaceful and benevolent, with no tides, sandbanks nor rocks to fuss about—a real yachtsman's paradise. Therefore it came as an unpleasant shock to find on our second day at sea, and Barbara's last day before returning to England, that it was littered with unexpected hazards and not at all the gentle sheet of water we had hoped for. The sea in the western end of the Baltic is very shallow and has hardly any salt in it, a combination which rapidly kindles an uncomfortably churned up and billowy effect in moderate breezes, and a positive maelstrom in strong winds. Another disturbing feature are the slender twigs surmounted by flimsy besoms which serve as channel-marking buoys in Denmark. If you happen to be staring straight into the midday sun with a wooded island beneath it, and a narrow passage through dangerous reefs to be negotiated before you can hope to reach that idyllic island harbour, there is always one urgent problem to be resolved: which, of that army of tree-trunks ahead, is the one and only tenuous stalk which may lead you to safety; or, at any rate, avert the chances of becoming a total wreck?

It was not until much later that I began to suffer from an anxiety complex caused by the strain of that type of navigation, day after day; however, Barbara and I had a foretaste, a nasty little hors-d'oeuvre, of what was to follow, during our nine-hour voyage from Sønderborg to Svendborg.

We crossed the Little Belt to AErø, then came to a difficult passage where we were compelled to tack into a fresh headwind with hardly any water under our keel and waves breaking on the reefs all around us. Just when I was beginning to lose all hope of reaching the other end without being pulverized on a rock, a tiny motor-cruiser appeared—it seemed to have dropped straight out of the sky—and led us safely across the reefs into the broader sound which runs north-eastwards to the beautiful town of Svendborg.

Barbara returned to England next day, as her children were expected home for their school holidays. We arranged that our final rendezvous in a month's time should be somewhere in the Gulf of Bothnia.

* * * * *

Svendborg has a splendid circular yacht harbour which was filled with Dragons and Folkboats and smiling yachtsmen, who seemed delighted to welcome an English Folkboat in their midst.

'You must go next to Omø,' said the young man on *F.B.* 305 next to *Martha*. 'You will *love* this pretty little island in our Great Belt.'

So I set off for Omø, but it was not until I had cleared the land next morning that I began to feel very much alone. It was quite different this time as I was in a strange country and could not speak a word of Danish, and I was not enthusiastic about my first impressions of navigation in the Baltic. But it was a perfect day, and I drifted gently along under mainsail and genoa wearing a swim-suit and trailing one foot over the side. The water was so clear that I could see every rock and jelly-fish beneath the hull, and the Danish countryside was very pretty with its pointed green hills and wooded shores, and an occasional blue-grey church spire or white windmill peeping over the trees.

The breeze died away before sunset, so I started the Seagull and motored across a glassy swell towards Omø. That invaluable book, *Den Danske Havnelods*, which gives details and small plans of every single harbour in Denmark, was clasped in my arms as I drew nearer to the island. However, on that occasion the harbour entrance eluded me as it was concealed by some fishing-net stakes running out to sea from the north coast. As a result, I motored right past it and struggled into a surprisingly strong current until I reached the rose-coloured lighthouse on the western extremity of Omø. Still no harbour and night approaching fast . . . what on earth should I do? And, suddenly, the miracle of the pilot-boat happened once again. This time it was a dinghy with an outboard motor which made for a clump of trees close to the stakes, then vanished from sight! I followed very cautiously with those hateful rocks, seemingly just below the surface of the water, glaring up at me; then a forest of masts appeared round a bend in the channel, and a tiny lighthouse on the end of a doll's sized breakwater. And there was Kirkehavn, the smallest harbour I had ever seen.

It was filled to the brim with large German yachts and at first glance there did not appear to be any mooring space left. But the skipper of an inter-island steamer took great trouble to make some room below the bows of his ship where, eventually, I was able to secure my lines. He seemed so kind and helpful that I offered him a glass of whisky, whereupon he descended briskly on to *Martha*'s stern and made himself very comfortable in the cockpit; he then proceeded to polish off the whole bottle with the assistance of one or two cronies who drifted towards us like moths towards a candle flame. I was hungry, tired and very bad-tempered by the time the cronies had drifted away into the night as there was nothing left for them to drink. The skipper lined up the empty bottle until it was exactly in transit with my angry face, then squinted at me with one eye half-closed and suggested that he should move into the cabin, as Omø, being a small island, was rather a gossipy place and we should be more private inside. I had just begun to fry some eggs over the stove, and I leapt out into the cockpit brandishing the sizzling pan over his head and told him to get off the boat before I threw him overboard! He did, much to my relief; so I hastily retreated into my lair and bolted the cabin door.

That night, as I lay in my bunk listening to a gaggle of drunks bawling profanities at some unfortunate boat on the far side of the harbour, I felt very homesick and wondered why I had ever had the urge to go to sea.

The following day was quite different. There was a fresh south-east wind blowing and I made very poor headway tacking into a steep breaking sea; but the sun shone brilliantly and the Danish islands looked very beautiful amid that blue and gold seascape with, here and there, a sailing coaster running before the wind under an ivory-coloured lugsail.

After eight hours hard tacking I had only gained sixteen miles and was wet, tired and hungry; so I made for the little island of Femø which was close at hand. The approach from the north is complicated by a shallow reef of sand and rocks, and I peered owlishly along the glaring sun-path through misty-wet spectacles, but not a hint of a broom-head could I see. However, there was nothing to worry about as my pilot-boat soon appeared round the southern tip of the island. This time it was a large Danish sailing-yacht, and by the time I reached the tiny square harbour of Femø—even smaller than Omø—she was already secured inside.

'*Velkommen!*' said a figure on the end of the jetty as I sailed in under mainsail alone.

'Thank you,' I gasped, struggling to haul down the sail before *Martha* had a chance to slice another boat in half: I was not yet accustomed to those pocket-handkerchief-sized harbours, and I made a mental note to tackle my arrivals with less drama and more discretion in the future!

Presently a Danish sea-scout joined the throng on the jetty above *Martha*, and told me in a broad American accent that his scout-master wished to place him at my disposal for shopping or any work I wanted to have done on the boat. So we went off shopping together and soon came to a charming little hamlet of white-washed cottages clustered around the one shop, which was already closed. But this made no difference as the scout was a friend of the woman who owned the shop, so she unlocked the back door and sold me all the things I needed.

Presently I returned to *Martha* and had just lit the stove for supper when a high-pitched squeaky voice called down to me, "Hello, Mees! Are you there?"

Through the half-opened hatch I could see a stalwart pair of legs clad in white woolly stockings, and as I climbed out into the cockpit a little woman with silvery-grey hair advanced and introduced herself as Sister Gertrud Möller of Faaborg, at present district nurse to the island of Femø. She told me that she had spent many happy holidays in England, and for this reason it had given her great pleasure to see a Red Ensign flying in Femø Harbour. I asked her aboard for a cup of coffee, but she said she would come back at nine o'clock as it was not good to delay my supper.

The wind dropped at sunset and it was a marvellous warm night with a full moon leading the eye along its shimmering path to the island of Fejø a few miles away. Later on the scout-master and his wife came along to see me, then Sister Möller returned and the helpful scout reappeared with a beautiful blonde girl-friend. We all sat on the harbour wall chatting quietly and looking out to sea, to where the anchor light of a Baltic trader glowed and flickered in the velvet night.

'What a difference to last evening!' I thought to myself. It seemed as if I had lived in Femø all my life, and I felt very happy sitting on the sea-wall with my new-found friends.

* * * * *

During the next two days the east wind blew harder than ever, combined with a falling barometer and frequent heavy squalls. The navigation through the winding channels between Sjælland, Falster and Møn, then along the Bøgestrøm and into the

Sue, Winkle and author as Wrens on naval pinnace

2 Author scrubbing decks—Nieuport, Belgium

Author working on *Imp* in winter quarters in Dover

4 *Imp* and author being towed past the Hurlingham Yacht Club

5 A busy day in the Pool of London

6   My cousin Gillian Maude—sailing into Ostende

7   Bernard, Alexandre and Robert aboard *Soeur Thérèse* off Dieppe

8   Margaret Boggis, who had also been a Leading Stoker in the W.R.N.S.

9   The men from the Ostende lifeboat attaching a hawser to *Imp*'s stern

10 *Martha McGilda* by Deryk Foster

11 Entering a small harbour on the Normandy coast could present quite a challenge in an onshore gale

12 Noel Jordan, the first owner of *Martha McGilda*

13 *Martha* and author in the tiny harbour of Femø

14 My first sight of Finland, the sinister black lighthouse of Marhällan

15 *Martha* at Simrisham, my favourite port in Sweden

20 The crew of the *Free Enterprise* on the top deck

21 Mother steering *Martha*

20   The crew of the *Free Enterprise* on the top deck

21   Mother steering *Martha*

9   Author collecting tickets from cars before they embarked on the *Free Enterprise* in Dover

16 *Martha* after her winter refit   17 *Martha* aground in Calais Harbour

18 A Dutch lifeboat in action off the Frisian Islands

15 *Martha* at Simrisham, my favourite port in Sweden

22 Captain J. E. Dawson, Master of M.V. *Free Enterprise*

23 *Roskilde* taking shape in McGruer's Yard

24 *Roskilde* takes to the sea for the first time—April 1974

25 *Roskilde* running before the wind

Peter Crago, John Munro and Victor Henry learning to sail *Martha* on the Thames

27 Captain Ian McLaren, our instructor at the School of Navigation

28 Texel out sailing in winter

29 Dick in mid-Channel

30 Waiting for his sea bird

Sound was like a nightmare. My course was south-east to begin with, then north-east, but whichever way I turned the wind moved round ahead of me. I tacked for hours on end towards the Storstrøm Bridge, the longest bridge in Europe, but the worst part of all came after the bridge, where there was a stretch of very shallow water sprinkled with wrecks, shifting banks and rocks embedded in sand. In some places the navigable channel narrows down to a width of thirty feet, and what with the perpetual tacking into a fresh wind, peering desperately ahead through bleary spectacles, trying to steer a compass course from one flimsy buoy to the next in case I failed to see them, and being soaking wet, hungry, thirsty and frightened, I began to long for a world in which there was no more sea, nor any boats!

Close to the Sjælland shore there was a new hazard in store for me in the shape of intermittent clumps of trees; *Martha* would suddenly get becalmed under their lee and I would start making a few optimistic preparations for lunch. Then a squall would hit us without any warning, laying the boat right over on her beam-ends for a few dreadful seconds.

During my passage through the Bøgestrøm I found myself racing against a German yacht, and had little difficulty in passing her despite the number of sail changes which her crew were ordered to make during a short space of time. She also was bound for Rødvig, a little town of white-washed cottages covered in rambler roses not far from Copenhagen. Later on that evening her owner came round to see me wearing an expression which reminded me of my maternal grandfather on the one unfortunate occasion when I succeeded in beating him at golf!

'*Guten abend, Fräulein!*' he growled, grasping my shrouds with puffy red fingers which looked as if they would rather have been round my neck. 'I vish you to know that the Engländer stole all our best *segel-jachten* at the end of the vorr!'

He spat viciously into the harbour and threw me another meaningful look which seemed to imply that I was personally responsible for what had happened; then he clicked his heels sharply together and marched back to his yacht.

Rødvig seemed to be full of German yachtsmen who nurtured

a particular hatred of everything Anglo-Saxon. This upset me a great deal as we had met such friendly people among the German Friesian Islands, and I remembered with special warmth the student off Baltrum who had offered to lend me his anchor.

I felt very tired and depressed that evening, and I was dimly aware that I had reached a difficult stage in the voyage. *Martha* was almost half-way to Helsinki and the novelty and glamour of the early days had worn off, and not yet been replaced by the excitement of drawing close to my objective. Also I was constantly obsessed with doubts about the various reasons for throwing up my job in London—where I had worked most happily for the past ten years—and setting off on this long and exacting challenge in pilotage and coastal navigation. The underlying reason, although I never admitted it to anyone, was that I had reached a rather gloomy crossroads in my life and desperately needed time and distance (from home) to get things into their right perspectives, and decide what to do next. And I was not at all sure, by the time I reached Rødvig, that I was getting any nearer to finding a solution.

There was a vile weather forecast and a rising east wind that night, so I slept for nearly two days; emerging refreshed from the cabin at the end of that time, I was befriended by a bearded Swede who lived with his wife and eight children aboard an old wooden boat which resembled Noah's Ark. He offered me a glass of schnapps and much useful information about his own country.

'Beware of Sandhammaren Point,' he stressed a number of times. 'It is a seaman's graveyard, that terrible place! Also do not sail with confidence into the Hanö-bukten, even if a soft wind beguiles you, for it is rightly named "The Bay of Storms".'

He then wrote out a list of small harbours in south-eastern Sweden which were deep enough for *Martha*'s four-foot draught. This proved invaluable in the next two weeks, as there was no Swedish pilotage book quite like *Den Danske Havnelods* at that time.

* * * *

I left Rødvig on July 21st and sailed across the Sound in mist and driving rain. There was a fresh north-west wind blowing that day and *Martha* sped across the grey seas on a broad reach, which made a welcome change from beating to windward. I had convinced myself that I should be able to see the Falsterborev Lightvessel and the coast of Sweden after two hours' sailing, but there was nothing in sight at the end of two and a half hours. There are dangerous shoals to the north of the lightvessel and in the Baltic, as I had already discovered, one seldom knows what strength of current is setting in which direction. How I longed for the North Sea that day, with its ordinary predictable rhythmic tides! I had worked myself up into a state bordering on hysteria when the lightvessel suddenly loomed up out of the mist, only a few yards ahead of me.

Trelleborg, my first Swedish harbour, turned out to be an ugly commercial port with no visible charm of any sort. But I sailed gaily towards it with my brand new Swedish courtesy flag fluttering from the port shrouds and a feeling of elation in my heart. What did it matter if the place was ugly? This was Sweden at last and the next country I would reach, God willing, would be Finland. And then I could send off that postcard to Monsieur Paul Luyten, way back in Nieuport!

Trelleborg turned out to be ugly in more ways than one. *Martha* had not long been secured in a quiet corner of the harbour, and I was sitting on the cabin-top doing some repairs to the mainsail when a cripple in a bath-chair arrived on the quay above me, accompanied by a group of Teddy Boys. They shared a number of jokes in husky chortles, then collected together some lumps of coal which were lying around on the quayside and began to hurl them down into *Martha*'s cockpit. I protested, without any marked success, so I retreated ignominiously into the cabin and bolted the door. There were a few more loud salvoes on the cabin-top, then they lost interest and wandered away.

After a hot and stuffy night, and further regrets about having set off on this crazy voyage, I woke feeling better and less intropective. Did all single-handers go through those waves of self-pity, I wondered?

Ystad, my second Swedish port, was the complete contrast. After a gentle sail along the coast of Skåne, which reminded me of Sussex with its rolling green hills to port and broad expanse of grey sea to starboard, I arrived at one of the oldest towns in Southern Sweden. Many of the buildings there date from the 12th century, and I wandered through a maze of narrow cobble-stoned streets where I found two ancient churches, the townhall, a beautiful monastery and some fine timbered houses; then I turned a sharp corner and rubbed my eyes to make sure that I was not dreaming for there, in front of me, stood a wooden pavilion surrounded by a green lawn, with a small orchestra performing on a raised dais in the middle of it. Each musician was clad in some brilliant-coloured operatic costume, and they struck up *Tales from the Vienna Woods* as I drew nearer. That fairy-tale scene was lit by Chinese lanterns, and there were small tables around the edge of the lawn where groups of people were drinking coffee—or was it nectar—and eating ambrosial cakes!

I had just sat down and ordered some myself, when a very embarrassing thing happened; an example, perhaps, of one of the main drawbacks to single-handed sailing, unless one is made of exceptionally tough fibre. I had been to collect my fortnightly mail from the local post office, an event which I looked forward to with joyful anticipation. However, on this occasion a letter from home brought the disturbing news that my dog had escaped one day and devoured a piglet's foot on a neighbouring farm, and the farmer was now threatening to shoot the dog. This upset me so much that I suddenly burst into tears and had to leave the coffee-garden very swiftly, and fade away into the lonely obscurity of the night streets. Looking back on the incident later, it seems an extraordinary thing to have done; but I supposed that the combination of lack of sleep, no regular meals, constant worries about the weather and navigation, and general homesickness had reduced me to the condition of a damp dish-mop!

The next day was 'Sandhammaren Day', a day which I had dreaded ever since my conversation with the bearded Swede in Rødvig. There was only a moderate north-east wind blowing, but it took me eleven miserable hours to sail round that fearsome point as there was an enormous sea, out of all proportion to the strength of the wind, running through the straits between

Bornholm and the Swedish coast. I tried using the Seagull in combination with the sails, but the engine was soon swamped by the waves so I hove to, hauled it back aboard and stowed it carefully away in its locker. It always gave me an uncomfortable feeling when the engine was not in a fit condition to use if it should suddenly be required, and I usually wrapped it up in tattered old jerseys and plastic bags to protect it from the water in the bilges.

It was a black starless night by the time I had sailed over the turbulent shoals which extend six miles southwards from Sandhammaren, and finally succeeded in passing the tall lighthouse on the end of the point. I was nearly at the end of my tether by then, not having eaten since early morning and wondering how on earth I should find my way into the nearest harbour before I collapsed at the helm. Then my pilot-boat suddenly appeared out of the darkness; a white fishing-boat from Bornholm which chugged straight across my course and led me safely in towards the land and through the tiny harbour entrance of Skillinge. A few minutes later I fell fast asleep fully dressed, with the steady choomph-a-choomph of powerful Diesel engines throbbing in my brain.

Next morning some aged fishermen ambled along the jetty to inspect my boat, and they helped me to fill the water-cans from the village pump. It was a friendly little place, and I felt a special warmth towards it when I noticed all the unlit buoys and fishing-net stakes just outside the harbour entrance, which I had narrowly missed hitting the night before!

There was a strong north wind blowing that day, so I sailed away from Skillinge under double-reefed mainsail and small jib, and took short tacks close inshore. Presently it began to rain; no gentle shower but a primeval downpour which beat straight into my face and down inside my oilskin collar. Before very long I was soaked to the skin, with chattering teeth, so I jumped up and down in the cockpit to try and keep warm, but this only served to hasten the formation of ice-cold puddles at the bottom of my sea-boots.

It was still pouring when I caught my first glimpse of Simrishamn, but nothing could detract from the beauty of that place. Even though my eyes were filled with rain-water I was immediately struck by the pastel-coloured houses round the harbour, the ancient church, the white fishing-boats and the sailing-coasters.

I moored *Martha* alongside a fine old sailing-ship called *Otelia* and I was in the middle of furling the soaking canvas mainsail when a magnificent harbourmaster, resplendent in a black uniform glittering with gold braid, leant over the bulwarks. He was accompanied by two damp-looking men wearing very squelchy brothel-creepers.

'Welcome to Simrishamn!' said the harbourmaster with a broad grin. 'Allow me to present these two gentlemen of the Swedish newspaper *Ystads Allehanda*. I have come as their interpreter.'

I shook hands with the gentlemen of the press, and a stream of water from the brim of my sou'wester descended on to their writing-pads. After answering a number of questions about my voyage, boat and family, the harbourmaster instructed me to look natural as the gentleman with the camera wished to photograph me. I assured him that I had seldom looked more natural in my life after six hours at sea in the Swedish rain! So the photographer flashed away quite happily, and I prayed that his camera might become water-logged.

Just before they left one of the reporters asked if he could see my navigational equipment. I showed him the two compasses —the hand-bearing one being my original prismatic compass I had bought when I was fourteen—an old pair of brass dividers, Captain Field's Improved parallel rules, my small radio for listening to the shipping forecasts, a number of pilotage books and a large bundle of charts.

'But where is your echo-sounder, your Walker Log, your direction finder, your transmitter for sending messages to the shore, and all the other things yachtsmen usually take to sea?' he demanded curiously.

'One would need a large crew to use and take care of all those complicated instruments,' I replied. 'If you have a good boat with a strong anchor, two reliable bilge-pumps, a compass which has no deviation, an excellent barometer and the other things I have just shown you, what more do you want?' Then I remembered my ancient leadline for testing the depths, but when I pulled it out of its locker both men peered at it as if they were being shown some relic from Noah's Ark.

The next day was my happiest day in Sweden. The sun was as bright as heaven and the west wind as warm and gentle as a loving embrace. I pegged all my wet clothes in the rigging to dry, and the grandson of Otelia's skipper climbed half way up her shrouds to get a better view into my cabin which must have been a rivetting experience, as he remained up there for over an hour! Then I went ashore to buy some postcards, and the woman in charge of the bookstall leant across the counter with the look of someone who was nursing a big joke and said, '*Blicka!*' And there was a hideous semblance of myself clinging to the mast in the pouring rain, on the front page of her newspaper.

During the afternoon various people climbed aboard *Otelia* and joined the skipper and his grandson, who stood on guard between me and the outside world. There was a fisherman from the Faeröes who had come along the coast from a distant village specially to see *Martha*, after reading about her in his morning paper. Then the school-master nephew of *Otelia*'s captain joined the party, and he took us all for a drive around the lovely old town. The twelfth-century church was the only one in Sweden, he told me, where a special carillon of bells was rung for the children on certain evenings during the year.

That evening we drove along the coast to the village of Vik where we dined on the terrace of a restaurant perched on a hillside, high above the sea. I vividly remember the tales told us by Svenning Guttesen, the Faeröese fisherman, about boats in the White Sea and the Denmark Strait fighting for their lives in the terrible winter storms in order to bring home a full cargo of fish: and, equally vividly, I remember the peace and enchantment of Vik, and the steak and fried potatoes and salad which tasted to me like food for the gods. Each time I turned my head to look out to sea, Svenning heaped my plate with a fresh helping of meat and vegetables and one of the others refilled my glass with wine.

Once again I was overwhelmed by the same feelings I had suffered from in Veere and in Femø; and I longed to stay in Simrishamn for ever and ever. But the sea was calm next morning and there was a fair wind blowing over the Hanö-bukten, so I said goodbye to all my new friends and put out to sea under full mainsail and genoa. When *Martha* had cleared the harbour entrance I looked back for a moment, and there was Svenning Guttesen and *Otelia*'s captain with his nephew and grandson, and the harbourmaster, all waving me goodbye. It seemed so sad to be sailing away, and I hastily opened the Baltic pilotage book to take my mind off the shore.

Some hours later the sky to the north began to turn the colour of ink. I rapidly changed the genoa for the small jib and took two reefs in the mainsail noticing, while I was clawing feverishly at the canvas, that there was a large Swedish yacht hove to a short distance ahead of me. I had never set eyes on her before, but I soon realized that she was waiting for me; and for the next four hours, during all the thunderstorms and heavy squalls which burst upon us, she stood close by me making valiant efforts to reduce her own speed. We were still sailing together at midnight when I turned off into the little harbour of Nögersund, as I was too worn out to go any further. We shouted goodbye to each other in the black squally night, and I never saw her again.

The entrance to Nögersund was bad enough, with a generous sprinkling of unlit beacons and waves pounding on barely concealed rocks, and the local fishing fleet pouring out of harbour to add to the general confusion. But it was child's play compared with the hair-raising close shaves *Martha* endured during the next few weeks in the archipelago. First there was the business of locating the *right* twig to lead me from the open sea into a narrow passage between millions of rocks and tiny islets and small islands covered in pine trees and little wooden houses. The wind was far too strong for my initiation to the skerries, and I sped through the inner leads at a most alarming speed; and, of course, there was no room to heave to and reduce some of the canvas, which can be another serious problem when sailing single-handed in the Baltic.

By the time I had reached the lovely yacht harbour near Karlskrona, the barometer had fallen below danger level and I was compelled to stay there for three days with a gale blowing, accompanied by torrents of rain. I began to feel very stuffy and down-hearted by the second day, sitting in *Martha*'s cabin drying wet clothes over the small paraffin stove and moving saucepans and balers around to catch the worst drips below-decks. Then I glanced out of one of the steamy portholes and noticed a police van drawing up at the end of the jetty. Presently a very large policeman stepped aboard and informed me that I was in a military zone and would not be allowed to leave!

'Don't be silly!' I protested anxiously. 'I *must* leave as soon as the weather improves; I'm days and days behind schedule already.'

I thought I detected a softening in his expression as he surveyed my damp surroundings and, perhaps, deduced that I was no great threat to the Swedish armed forces. Anyhow he offered me a lift into Karlskrona to get an official permit from the naval authorities, then drove me back to the yacht harbour and said goodbye with a click of the heels.

After Karlskrona I crept slowly and unhappily across a dreadful sheet of water called the Östra Fjärden, which was infested with tiny islets, rocks and shoals. What with the rain beating into my face, then losing my way completely during one of the brief intervals when I had taken my glasses off to wipe them, I arrived in Torhamn feeling like a neurotic and saturated mouse. The *Ystads Allehanda* had described me as 'that audacious female navigator who faces our Swedish skerries without a tremor!', and I felt relieved that one of their representatives was not awaiting my arrival in Torhamn that evening.

After Torhamn, I sailed for days and days through the Swedish skerries, slowly inching my way north across the small-scale chart of the Baltic until I reached the jumping-off point for Finland. I made friends with a Finnish family on a white ketch called *Ragni*, and we sailed together for nearly a week, up the long narrow Kalmarsund and on to the little town of Västervik.

When the weather was fine it was very beautiful in that world of smooth-faced rocks, with blood-red wooden houses nestling among tall pine trees and rowing-boats moored in sheltered coves below them, and tiny white lighthouses perched on rocky promontories at the cross-roads of the meandering channels. Each evening I selected a natural harbour and, sailing boldly into the middle of it, I threw the anchor over the stern then advanced cautiously towards a rock where I would leap ashore and attach the bow-line to the trunk of a tree. Then I scrambled back aboard and gave a sharp tweak to the anchor chain, which brought *Martha* back into the middle of our own private harbour. Towards evening the wind was usually no more than a gentle sigh in the upper branches of the trees, while the long green shadows drew out across the still water. Yes, it was certainly a bewitching coastline with its dancing sunlit skerries in the daytime and its silent peaceful nights; but there were times when I harboured a fierce longing for the harsh salty smell of the North Sea and the squawking of a big Dover seagull.

On August 24th *Martha* reached the small island of Furusund, north-east of Stockholm, and I was delayed there for eight days in a fierce northerly gale. The temperature dropped very suddenly, so I packed away my swim-suit and dressed myself in several layers of winter clothing instead. It really was very bleak on that island and the few people I met regaled me with harrowing tales of shipwrecks and disasters out in the Gulf of Bothnia. I became more and more depressed and anxious about reaching Helsinki before the Finnish winter set in.

During the last two days of the gale I noticed that the wind tended to drop a little after sunset and freshen up to its full fury by nine or ten next morning. Bearing this in mind, I left Furusund at daybreak on September 1st, and sailed down to the outer edge of the skerries where I dropped anchor in a natural harbour to wait for nightfall. I tried to get some rest before the night crossing, but found it quite impossible to relax and ignore the menacing sound of the wind roaring across the outer skerries.

Towards evening I layed off a number of courses on the chart, and sat in the cockpit for some while trying to memorise the exact positions of all the unlit buoys and beacons and half-submerged rocks along the route. The wind had certainly dropped and backed farther north, but some ominous black clouds were gathering around the edges of a lurid orange sunset and the barometer had begun to fall again.

I made a stew from one of my favourite Swedish tins, '*Kot Bullar*'; but it merely stuck in my throat and did not make me feel any better. I had decided to leave at midnight so that I might hope to reach the outer edge of the Åland archipelago just after daybreak. Accordingly, at 11.30 p.m. I put on several layers of woolly garments, and finally struggled into my oilskins and sea-boots. All the warmth of summer had been blown away during the past week, and it was an inky-black night and just beginning to rain. Next I lit the navigation lamps and fixed them in their brackets on the pulpit: there was no sign of a light from any human habitation or passing vessel, and my little harbour seemed the loneliest and most desolate spot I had ever seen.

Inside the cabin the warm glow of the stove and the oil lamp made the outside world seem infinitely remote. Presently the rain began to beat down on the deck with a steady persistence, and I found myself thinking 'Now or never, which is it to be?' But I knew, instinctively, that there was really no question of turning back, so I leapt into action, glad to be fully occupied at last. I hoisted the mainsail, but no jib, so that I might have a better view of any unforeseen dangers in the murky night. Then I hauled in the anchor and, with the aid of compass bearings and my biggest torch shining on the rocks, I crept safely out into the main channel leading from Stockholm to the open sea.

The two great lighthouses of Tjärven and Söderarm beckoned *Martha* towards them, and suddenly I felt a strange thrill of excitement as we stole silently through the skerries on that cold wet night. Shortly after 2 a.m. the lighthouses were abeam of us—four blinding flashes to starboard and a double occulting light to port—and *Martha* began to rise and fall on the back of a steadily increasing swell. The wind was freshening again and it was bitterly cold.

At last we were out in the Gulf of Bothnia with all the Swedish rocks behind us. A big sea was still running after the seven-day gale and, to add to my problems, there was a magnetic anomaly caused by deposits of iron ore on the sea-bed in that area which made the compass totally unreliable. It was a horrible night passage, what with the freezing-cold rain, the waves rearing up out of the darkness and the extreme uncertainty of my position; but the miserable hours dragged slowly by and just as the pale fingers of dawn began to touch the eastern horizon, I spotted Nyhamn light away on the starboard bow.

'Thank God, we're on the right course after all, and only a

few more miles to go!' I told *Martha*. The relief was so intense that I felt drained of all strength and incentive and, flopping down on the cockpit floor, I closed my eyes for a few seconds while my boat steered towards the dawn.

Presently I picked out the sinister black lighthouse of Märhallen dead ahead. I crawled precariously across the heaving cabin-top and hauled down the faded Swedish flag with fingers which were numbed with cold. What a splendid moment it was when I hoisted the brand new Finnish one in its place! I celebrated by opening a Thermos of hot coffee which I had made the night before and adding a few drops of whisky to it; then I drank a special toast to *Martha* and lingered over that heavenly warming liquid, which helped to restore the circulation to my frozen hands and feet.

Before long the sun broke through a bank of stormy-looking clouds and the wind hardened rapidly. *Martha* sped towards the islands as if she had been there before and could hardly wait to renew her acquaintance with them. At 8.30 a.m. we sailed triumphantly into Mariehamn harbour and moored alongside a small jetty behind the four-masted barque, *Pommern*.

Mariehamn, the home of the great shipbuilder, Gustav Erikson, was a place I had longed to visit since my earliest childhood. For years I had dreamt of all those glorious square-rigged ships sailing out of that very same harbour, and had sensed the romance which attached to that proud group of islands where the women and children farmed the land while their menfolk wrested a living from the stormy seas. Even today the Åland flag flies defiantly from the flagstaff of many a fine ship.

I was happily daydreaming in the cockpit when my first visitor arrived. He was a man of strikingly nautical appearance —perhaps the spirit of Gustav Erikson himself—and he walked briskly along the jetty and stopped just above *Martha*.

'Allow me to welcome you to Finland!' he said, treating the boat to a careful scrutiny. 'For a long time the *Pommern* has been the most famous ship in Mariehamn, but today there is another ship more famous still, and her name is *Martha McGilda*!'

Suddenly I knew that the long hard struggle to sail to Finland had been worthwhile, and I felt so emotional that I could have leapt ashore and hugged the man! After breakfast I rushed into the town to buy a postcard to send to Monsieur Paul Luyten, nearly 2,000 miles away in Nieuport. The great moment had at last arrived.

* * * * *

Barbara came back to join me for the last lap of the voyage, and we had a fast and exhilarating sail across the Åland Sea and along the south coast of Finland. In Helsinki we were told that the ship on which our return passage had been booked, had already left to load timber at Kotka, near the Finno/Russian frontier; so we pursued her through the rugged skerries of Eastern Finland and passed close to the Russian island of Suursaari. At last I was able to hoist my Russian courtesy flag.

A few days later Barbara, *Martha* and I returned to England aboard the *Baltic Express*; a voyage of only four days, whereas it had taken me over three months outward bound under sail!

8. A NIGHT TO REMEMBER

Brixham town lay quietly sleeping in the cold grey dawn. The late night revellers had all gone home and the milkmen had not yet started on their rounds; but out in the harbour the yachts pitched and tossed fretfully at their moorings, and already the first fishing-boats were getting under way. The wind had backed round to the north-east during the night, and a big swell came rolling in from Torbay. It was the thirteenth of August, and I woke up with an unpleasant hollow sensation in the pit of my stomach . . .

Ever since my voyage to the Baltic I had dreamt of making a longer sea passage—nothing too dramatic; say sixty to a hundred miles out of sight of land—just to prove that I was no longer a total sea-mouse! And at last the great moment had arrived.

I had sailed to Torbay that summer to see the start of the Tall Ships' Race, and the day after their departure I found myself teetering on the brink of that self-imposed ordeal, which had cast a dark shadow over the whole of my summer holiday: I was about to set off on a single-handed passage of eighty-five miles, from Brixham to Cherbourg. The morning shipping forecast gave north-easterly winds, Force 3 to 4, and no major depressions near the western end of the Channel. Apart from the fact that it was the thirteenth day of the month, everything

A Night to Remember

seemed auspicious for crossing to France. I hastily made some coffee and boiled an egg, but had great difficulty in swallowing it; I then hoisted the sails, cast off my mooring ropes and sailed reluctantly out of Brixham Harbour.

The sea was uninvitingly grey and choppy in Torbay, and I was compelled to take a long tack north-westwards to clear Berry Head. Half an hour later I came about on to the port tack and settled down on a course of 130° Magnetic, straight towards Cherbourg. *Martha* skimmed across the waves in fine style, her jib and the lower half of her mainsail already soaked with spray. I was wearing five pullovers, two pairs of trousers and submarine socks under my oilskins and sea-boots, but I did not feel particularly warm or comfortable. Most of the time I sat hunched over the tiller, firmly wedged into one corner of the cockpit, afraid to take my eyes off the compass for more than a few seconds. This was quite a new experience for me, not being able to steer towards any fixed object on the horizon ahead.

At midday I noted in the log-book that the wind was E.N.E. 4 and the sea distinctly choppy. I had just passed a pair of French trawlers which gave me a false glimmer of hope, as I imagined that I must have crossed the Channel at some miraculous speed and already be approaching the French coast. But a few brief calculations soon dispelled that fantasy. During the afternoon the sun broke through the clouds and the sea became quite blue. I began to feel more cheerful, and the sight of some seagulls planing over the crests of the waves made that empty heaving seascape seem less lonely.

This optimistic mood continued for several hours, until I switched on the shipping forecast at five to six. It appeared that a depression had turned in its tracks and was rapidly approaching Sea Area Portland, with winds expected to strengthen from the east during the night. I crawled into the cabin and tapped the barometer; it fell about three millibars while I crouched there gaping at it.

About this time a curious shape loomed up on the southern horizon. 'Surely that must be Alderney,' I told myself with returning confidence; 'I'll make for there instead of Cherbourg.'

I took a good swig of rum and devoured some ginger biscuits, then pulled out the charts of Alderney and the Channel Pilot,

Volume II, and studied them in great detail. This proved to be a sobering experience as I read of swift-flowing tidal streams, outlying rocks, a submerged breakwater at the entrance to Braye Harbour, whirlpools, overfalls and countless other hazards. I looked towards the south again, and the shape which I thought was Alderney had risen into the sky, being no more than a bank of dark clouds. The evening began to draw in and suddenly I felt very cold and frightened, and very much alone.

I was sailing close to the wind which had veered east and increased to Force 5 by that time. With the approaching darkness I decided to heave to, take two reefs in the mainsail and light the navigation lamps. Once that was done I put *Martha* on course again, and studied the damp charts of Alderney by torch-light. I was not at all sure of my position after twelve hours at sea.

About nine o'clock I picked up Alderney Light and the five flashes every thirty seconds from the great lighthouse on the Casquets. My spirits rose like a thermometer held under a hot water tap, and I pictured myself safely moored in Braye Harbour, cooking a tasty supper in the warm cosy cabin. I freed the sheets and altered course towards Alderney Lighthouse, and the boat surged through the confused breaking seas which reared up out of the twilight. Presently the dark outline of the island appeared on the starboard bow, and I could just make out a few pinpricks of light around Braye Harbour. I was not sure where to look for the entrance lights as I had never been there before.

Suddenly *Martha* refused to answer to the helm. I sawed the tiller to and fro, but she swung wildly up into the wind, then right back towards the Casquets, almost causing me to gybe. I thought the rudder must have broken, and my mind went racing back to the *Imp* on our first attempt to cross the Channel. I hung helplessly over the stern with my arms clasped round the backstays, shining a torch down into the heaving black water. What a relief! The rudder was still there. Then it occurred to me that we had just passed through a whirlpool; a speciality of the Channel Islands to which I had not been exposed for some years.

Martha drew quite close to Braye Harbour and gigantic

A Night to Remember

hissing waves bombarded her from all directions. The west-flowing tide was just beginning to gather momentum. The moon rose up from behind a battlement of black clouds, and I could see rocks the size of cathedral spires sticking up out of the water away to the west; and, furthermore, I could hear the thunder of the waves breaking on the rocks. I could also see the outline of the breakwater by then, but could not find the leading lights. Despite the strength of the wind, the tide was slowly and surely pushing me westwards along the island, away from the harbour entrance. Suddenly a voice—perhaps Noel Jordan's—seemed to say to me: 'Stop being a plumb stuffed idiot! Get out to sea and wait for the tide to turn and the dawn to break; then, at least, you might be able to *see* where the entrance lies.'

I put *Martha* about on to the starboard tack, pulled in the sheets and headed northwards into the wild tumultuous darkness. I felt unutterably tired, miserable and pessimistic. Some two or three hours later I hove to and dropped off to sleep in the cockpit. All my clothes were soaking wet, my boots filled with sea-water, my torch water-logged and useless and my charts reduced to a mass of pulp. Nevertheless, I slept, hugging the tiller with both arms.

Suddenly I was wide awake with a brilliant light shining right into my face. It was the light from the Casquets Lighthouse, a gaunt and terrifying structure towering over me in the ragged moonlight, only a few yards away. I let fly the jib sheet, rammed the tiller hard over and the boat responded in the nick of time; she clawed her way out towards the open sea with the ugly fangs of rocks, which had so nearly devoured us, slowly dropping astern. After that experience there was no more heaving to or falling asleep. I sailed hard to windward for the next four hours, making very little headway against the strong wind and tide. The barometer fell steadily.

At four o'clock in the morning the tide began to slacken and it was pouring with rain. The first glimmer of dawn, however, was beginning to lighten the eastern sky. Some while later the rain turned to hailstones; then, quite suddenly, a gale blew straight out of the east; 'the sector of hope', as I had christened it, from which I was eagerly awaiting enough light to guide me into Alderney Harbour. Mountainous waves crashed aboard every few seconds, and I could hear the water swilling from side to side in the cabin as I clung to the tiller for dear life.

I turned towards the south wearing the baler, like a French beret, over one eye to protect my face from the driving hailstones and blinding salt spray. I let out the mainsheet to shake some of the wind out of the sail; aloft it behaved like some demented thundering demon, but we rode the huge seas a bit easier.

It was almost daylight. I could still just see Alderney Light when we rose on the crest of a wave, and I prayed that the lighthouse-keeper would not switch it off too soon, before I had had a chance to find the harbour entrance. *Martha* came surging in towards the island once again, and for a few brief minutes I forgot all my tiredness and fear; all the usual mouselike sentiments were replaced by a glorious feeling of exhilaration and complete confidence in my boat.

We rounded the submerged breakwater and ran before the gale into Braye Harbour, narrowly missing a crop of rocks on our port hand. I looked them up on the chart some days later, and noticed that they protruded from the foot of Roselle Point. Quite a dramatic ending that might have been!

* * * * *

By the end of the week I had recovered sufficiently to sail back to Dover via the Normandy coast, calling at nearly every harbour en route. Instead of throwing off the sea-mouse image after my crossing from Brixham to Alderney, I found that nothing had altered and I was right back to square one!

'What are you trying to prove,' I asked myself, 'when you *know* that you have a good boat, and you certainly do *not* enjoy being at sea in a gale? Anyway, what's so wonderful about single-handed sailing? And what do the people who earn their livings on the sea think of all these crazy yachtsmen?'

9. ANOTHER KIND OF SAILING

One cold winter's evening the following year I had an unexpected visit from an old sailing friend, Dr Brian Woodward, who lived with his family in the village of Lyminge near Folkestone. Brian owned a Folkboat similar to *Martha,* and was planning a short voyage along the French coast in April, so he had come over to propose that we should cross to Calais in company. Another doctor, who had been a friend of Brian's since their student days, was with him that evening, and he had been invited to go as crew on *Ken-Fyne* on the trip to France.

I remember feeling rather annoyed at the sudden interruption to whatever I was doing, which seemed very important at the time. And my little spaniel behaved in the most extraordinary way. I had placed Brian and his friend, Dick, in the best armchairs and poured them out glasses of beer, and the scene was all set for a quiet discussion of tides, compass courses and other details. But Bonzo decided otherwise; he sat very close to Dick's feet, staring at him fixedly with bloodshot angry-looking eyes and growling incessantly. It was not until I had removed the animal and shut him up in the kitchen, that we were able to spread out our charts on the floor and make our plans in peace.

* * * * *

We changed our arrangements when the time came, as Brian had sailed to Calais in a race the previous week-end and decided to leave his boat over there until the holiday started, so he and Dick returned to France by ferry and I sailed across in *Martha* alone.

I left Dover at eight o'clock in the morning, and there was a fresh south-west wind blowing up the Channel which caused a vicious snarling sea outside the eastern entrance. I felt cold and rather frightened, but soon gleaned some comfort from an unexpected glimpse of the French coast only a few minutes after leaving harbour.

An hour or so later the sun came out and the sea grew calmer and blue-green, with islands of floating seaweed drifting peacefully by. Suddenly I felt very happy to be at sea again, and I inhaled deeply because the breeze smelt of crude salt and vintage wine and the best life of all away from the land. *Martha* sang her own special song as the bows cleft a path through the sparkling waves, and I felt convinced that she shared my feelings after her dreary winter of idleness in harbour.

Four hours later we sailed into the port of Calais, between the two long breakwaters where fishermen were tending big square nets along the cat-walks, their faces furrowed with deep concentration and the weathering of many storms. And there was *Ken-Fyne*, Brian's boat, rolling gently in the anchorage outside the Bassin de l'Ouest.

I began to tack across the harbour towards the other Folkboat, but had not sailed very far before *Martha* ran aground on the edge of a sandbank. It was an infuriating situation as the tide was still falling, and having made a successful landfall I had been intent on sailing rather stylishly across the port of Calais! To make matters worse Brian and his friend suddenly appeared outside the yacht club and offered me some navigational advice which, by then, I was too late to profit from.

Presently *Martha* began to heel over towards the shore and, sooner than face any further embarrassments, I crept into the cabin like a badger seeking its lair and attempted to warm up a saucepanful of soup over the heavily tilted stove. After a while I began to feel very drowsy so I wedged myself into the bunk on the landward side and fell fast asleep.

Two hours later the tide was flooding hard, and I awoke with a start when the boat began to right herself and grind her keel on some shingle. Although she was almost afloat the wind was blowing her farther up on to the bank all the time, quite close to some jagged-looking rocks. Observing my hazardous position, Dick jumped into *Ken-Fyne*'s dinghy and rowed across to take my C.Q.R. anchor out on a hefty length of rope. That solved the problem and I was soon able to pull *Martha* off the bank.

We had agreed to leave Calais on the north-going tide that afternoon and sail in company further up the coast; our final destination was to be Nieuport in Belgium. *Martha* and *Ken-Fyne* weighed anchor simultaneously at four o'clock, and because neither boat wished to appear more cautious than the other, we both hoisted our full mainsails and working jibs. There was a fresh southerly wind blowing out at sea by then, and fierce green waves broke in clouds of spray over the Ridens de la Rade and the bows of the two hard-pressed Folkboats. All the same I felt like bursting into song with the sheer exhilaration of our headlong progress, and it was a rare treat to be sailing along like that within a stone's throw of another boat. I was conscious of a warm safe feeling, quite different from the loneliness of single-handed sailing without another ship in sight.

We steered well clear of the treacherous sandbanks on which the Walde Light stands sentinel, and two hours later we crossed the bar into the narrow mouth of the River Aa, which flows two miles inland until it reaches the old walled town of Gravelines.

The wind was blowing straight down the river towards us, so we started our engines, furled our sails and motored in single file along the channel past the twin fishing villages of Grand and Petit Fort Philippe. There was a black and white striped lighthouse on the left-hand side, very compact and workmanlike on the outskirts of the village; and on the opposite bank I noticed some sturdy black fishing-boats aground on the mud, with a cluster of picturesque houses and a bistro called the Café Jacqueline rising above them. This was the hamlet of Grand Fort Philippe, and just as we came abreast of the landing-stage a primeval ferry pushed off from the shore; an old man in faded blue dungarees was sculling with a long oar over the stern and a nun sat motionless and bolt upright on the bow thwart. For a few seconds the ferry, the recumbent fishing-boats and the houses above were all reflected faithfully in the still grey water; then it began to rain and the surface of the river was pitted with a thousand tiny craters.

Eventually we reached the lock which leads into the quiet little Bassin Vauban at Gravelines, and passed through it at the same time as a large German coaster from Hamburg. By the time we had moored both boats alongside the wall the wind was coming in great gusts off the land, and the scent of rich pastures mingled with the driving rain.

Brian poured out three large tumblers of gin and tonic inside *Ken-Fyne*'s cabin, which seemed as warm and cosy as a thrush's nest after the last hour or so at sea. My eyelids soon began to droop, so I climbed back on to *Martha* and fell asleep while Brian and Dick went ashore to find a restaurant for dinner.

* * * * *

The wind was blowing a full gale from the north-west next morning, so we decided to spend the day in Gravelines. Situated half way between the busy ports of Calais and Dunkerque, it is a sleepy little place with a certain old-world charm. Very few cars or lorries disturb the peaceful atmosphere of the narrow cobblestoned streets, for Gravelines has been by-passed by the bustling locomotion of the twentieth century.

We spent a pleasant enough day pottering on our boats, lunching ashore, shopping and listening to all the shipping forecasts. That evening it was my turn to be hostess to Brian and Dick. I lit the oil lamp and candles in *Martha*'s little cabin, set up the table (which is only used for special occasions) and prepared a supper consisting of beef and onion stew, followed by a rich plum cake, cheese and biscuits, and a bottle of vin rosé to accompany the food. The meal was undoubtedly a success, and we were all feeling cheerful and rested after a quiet day in harbour. The rain had stopped and the wind seemed less boisterous, so we decided to walk to the little fishing village of Grand Fort Philippe to have a few drinks at the Café Jacqueline, which we had noticed on our passage in from the sea the previous afternoon.

Another Kind of Sailing

The time was nine o'clock when we set off along the left bank of the River Aa, leading down towards the coast. It was a lovely night with half a moon shining and the smell of wet hay strong and pungent up to windward. The path ran along the top of a high bank with the river below us on one side and a great field, which might have been a pale green expanse of the sea, below us on the other side. We walked on and on, with the occulting light at Petit Fort Philippe growing bigger and bigger all the time. I felt inspired by the bracing night air and could have walked for miles, but Brian and Dick did not share my enthusiasm as they were wearing heavy sea-boots.

Presently we came to the outskirts of Grand Fort Philippe. The little houses were dark and silent, their reflections dimly visible in the murky surface of the half-tide river. I could see the silhouettes of fishing-boats aground on the mud, and a large building with Dutch gables which turned out to be the home of the lifeboat; but not a light shone in any of the houses, and an oppressive stillness engulfed the whole place.

Eventually we spotted a red neon sign announcing the Café Jacqueline and heard the sound of music inside. We pushed open the door and stood there for a moment to savour the warm bright interior, which contrasted so strongly with the dark silent village outside.

Brian bought the first round of drinks, and in a short while we had been absorbed into a friendly group of youths who insisted on treating us to the next round and offering us their cigarettes at frequent intervals. Several of them were merchant seamen, and one in particular made a strong impression on me because of his darkly truculent face. He showed me the photograph in his Seaman's Record Book with great pride, and boasted a good deal about his voyages to South Africa and the Far East in a big freighter from Dunkerque.

The bar was presided over by a sharp-featured woman with a masterful personality, and the atmosphere inside the café was thick with the fumes of Gaulloise tobacco, raw garlic and Pernod, with the harsh accents of Northern France cutting through it like a rip-saw.

Half an hour later the group of youths who had included us in their circle announced that they were going to a dance in the village-hall, and they invited us to join them. We refused as Brian was anxious to get back to *Ken-Fyne* before midnight in order to hear the late-night shipping forecast.

The seamen left and, simultaneously, a party of local fishermen accompanied by some wild-looking women came in and sat down in a corner of the café. A few minutes later the seamen returned, very surly and bad-tempered, as the dance had come to an abrupt end as soon as they walked into the hall. Suddenly the Café Jacqueline began to look rather sinister, and we all felt it was time to leave. We finished our drinks without appearing to hurry, and one of the seamen insisted on each of us accepting a final cigarette from him as we stood up to go. We shook hands with everyone in the approved French manner and wished them all goodnight, but as soon as we had stepped outside into the street Brian crossed to the other side and threw his Gaulloise cigarette into the river. I remember hoping that no one inside the café had seen him.

We started to walk back through the silent village, and a few minutes later we were out in the open country with the turbid black river on our left and the pale green field on our right. A broad beam from the lighthouse at Petit Fort Philippe swept across the night landscape every few seconds, and there was a cold damp wind blowing in from the sea coast.

Presently we heard several pairs of footsteps running along the path behind us, so we all moved to the left to allow whoever was in such a hurry to pass. Then, quite suddenly, it started without a word of warning. . . . Seven or eight big cowardly thugs attacked Brian and Dick from all sides at once, bashing them on the head and kicking them with heavy sea-boots once they were down. I was so astonished that I just stood there like a useless dummy, clutching my handbag under one arm and kicking feebly with one foot whenever the chance occurred. I recognized some of our new acquaintances from the Café Jacqueline and tried to reason with them, but they merely spat at me and said all the English were *salauds*.

Brian was shouting and swearing at his attackers, and letting fly with all his might; but he was hopelessly outnumbered and one of the youths landed two terrific blows on either side of his head which knocked him right out. He rolled off the path, over and over, down towards the field; at that point there was a gap in the lower half of the fence and he rolled right under it and finished up in a bed of spring cabbages. I stood on top of the bank observing everything minutely, but frozen into a state of hopeless immobility. I began to wonder if it would be my turn next.

About that time I suddenly became aware of what was happening to Dick. He had the mildest cornflower-blue eyes and a very gentle nature, but there he was a few yards away from me, tackling four of the biggest thugs all at once. He was right over on the left-hand side of the path and I was terrified of them knocking him unconscious then pushing him down the bank into the river. However, at that moment he seemed to have floored one of his opponents and had just landed on top of him on the grass verge, when another man came up from behind and kicked his head with a sea-boot so hard that he could not raise it any more. Then the pack closed in and began to pummel him on the ground. I took one more look at him with his face all covered in blood, then I slid down the bank to search for Brian in the field.

In my frantic haste I could not find the hole in the fence, so I ran along the ditch until I came to a house, then through their yard and back into the field. Brian was wandering around in a dazed manner, holding his head in both hands and muttering incoherent phrases. I led him back through the yard, all the time urging him to hurry and trying to explain what was happening to Dick; but when we reached the path the whole gang had suddenly vanished. Shortly afterwards poor Dick crawled up the bank and limped slowly towards us; he was covered in blood, his nose broken and one of his ankles sprained. Brian and I supported him as best we could for the remainder of the walk back to Gravelines. When at last we reached the Bassin Vauban there was a fat policeman on night-duty near the timber wharves, so we made our way across to where he was standing to report the attack. He cleared his throat noisily once or twice, looked to the right and the left of us like a cornered rabbit and said that he was desolated to hear what we had to tell him, but on no account must we derange ourselves as it was assuredly some Germans from the coaster who had attacked us!

After which he turned and spat into a pile of timber and growled something which sounded like '*Les sales Bosches*'. We left him at that point, and I helped the two men to climb painfully aboard *Ken-Fyne*.

I made some coffee in *Martha*'s cabin and Brian managed to drink a little but Dick was feeling too sick to touch it. Later on Brian set his nose for him and strapped up his ankle. I soon realised how lucky it was that they were both doctors.

I hardly slept that night, what with worrying about my two companions and wondering whether we should be attacked again. Suddenly our peaceful little sailing trip had turned into a sort of nightmare, and within the space of a few hours we all seemed to have grown about ten years older. The following morning Brian complained that his head was hurting very badly and Dick had two immense black eyes, any number of cuts and bruises and a swollen painful nose, but he assured us that Brian had made a good job of the setting.

I found myself wondering what sort of person he really was. Up till the previous night I had vaguely classified him as 'the man who little Bonzo growled at!' And quite unexpectedly he had emerged as a valiant giant with an infinitely hard core of resistance hidden beneath a mild and peace-loving disposition.

* * * * *

We only had two days left before we were due back at work again (Dick was working at a hospital in Hitchin at that time), and it was clear to us all that we should not have time to sail to Belgium. Brian decided to ring up Commandant Couliou, the Captain of the French ferry, *Côte d'Azur*, who was a good friend of ours, and he and his wife leapt straight into their car and drove straight to the Bassin Vauban. He insisted on reporting the attack to the Chief of Police in Gravelines, and also on taking us back to the Café Jacqueline to try and identify some of the thugs.

It was a weird sensation returning there in broad daylight, with the sun shining on the quaint little houses and the black fishing-boats. The Patronne of the café, who had only moved to Grand Fort Philippe a few months ago, gave a convincing impression of wishing to help us. Nevertheless, when the dark

Another Kind of Sailing

truculent-looking seaman, who had been one of Dick's worst assailants, came in and noticed us sitting there with the Coulious, he swiftly faded away and was nowhere to be seen when we ran to the door.

Our French friends questioned a number of people in Grand Fort Philippe but no one knew of the existence of any of the youths we described...

'Assuredly they were not of this neighbourhood,' vouched one old crone with evil squinting black eyes. 'One is pulverized with foreigners in this village nowadays, what with the swiftness of modern locomotion and the packet-boats arriving daily in Calais and Dunkerque!'

There seemed to be little point in lingering there any longer, so we drove back to Gravelines where Brian and Dick had to fill in detailed statements at the police station. While they were busy writing, the Chief of Police told me that he was completely desolated that we should have formed such a bad opinion of his town, but one had to realize that the inhabitants of Grand Fort Philippe were not like other people as they were descendants of the Barbary Corsairs! Apparently they had landed on that part of the coast some hundreds of years ago and settled in the twin fishing villages at the mouth of the River Aa.

As soon as all the official statements had been completed the Coulious set off back to Calais. Brian, Dick and I returned to our boats and moved them alongside the German coaster, which gave us a feeling of added security for the coming night. We had curry and rice for supper aboard *Ken-Fyne*, then turned in very early.

The wind dropped during the night and the early morning forecast announced a light south-westerly breeze and a calm sea, so we cleared the lock at Gravelines soon after breakfast and hoisted our mainsails and genoas. *Martha* and *Ken-Fyne* sailed rather splendidly, one behind the other, down the River Aa towards the sea. Their sails were goose-winged because the wind was blowing from dead astern, and not a sound came from either boat apart from the swish and slap of the murky river flowing past their clinker-built hulls. I noticed that the ferry worked by the old man in his faded blue dungarees was about to push off from the shore but, except for him, the hamlet of

Grand Fort Philippe appeared to be deserted; all the younger descendants of the Barbary Corsairs had gone to ground.

* * * * *

The day we sailed back to England was the most perfect day in the whole year. The sun shone down on us out of a sapphire blue sky and the sea glittered and sparkled with gold and silver lozenges; and away on the far horizon there was a dark blue line which merged gently back into the paler blue sky.

The breeze was very light and fitful, and at the end of six hours we were still sailing northwards with no landmarks or seamarks in sight to tell us where we were. Then the wind died away completely, so Brian started his engine and took me in tow. Some while later the East Goodwin Lightvessel appeared on the starboard bow, and there were scores of large freighters crossing our course as we were right in the middle of the main north-going shipping lane.

We altered course towards the South Goodwin Lightvessel and the strong spring tide carried us triumphantly along on its back. The sun sank into a bed of purple and gold clouds away towards Dungeness and all the lights came on, one by one. It was the magic hour, the time of the afterglow, when the last dying embers of the twilight merged imperceptibly with the first shades of the young night.

Brian and Dick sat on the stern of *Ken-Fyne* drinking tumblers of gin and tonic and singing *The Keeper of the Eddystone Light* at the tops of their voices, and I sat on *Martha*'s stern drinking rum and orange and watching the great beam of the South Foreland light beckoning me home.

It was quite dark by the time we had picked up our moorings in the Camber and rowed ashore. Bobby Melhuish, the G.P. from St Margaret's Bay, was doing a few jobs on his boat with his daughter when we sailed into harbour, and he offered the three of us a lift back home. His car was an ancient Ford Popular, but everyone managed to squeeze into it in their heavy sailing clothes and I found a comfortable seat at the back in the half-open boot. The moon was shining brightly as we set off up the steep hill past Dover Castle, and there were strong earthy smells wafting into my nostrils from the evening fields.

The wind of our passage blew my hair into rough tangled streamers, and a premonition of some enormous happiness seemed to fill my whole being as the car bumped up and down on the winding road over the cliffs. And that was how we came safely home from the sea . . .

10. I JOIN THE MERCHANT NAVY

I leant over the ship's side to watch a rainbow in the bow wave, a marvellous iridescent arc dancing up and down over the sombre grey seas in the Dover Strait. Suddenly I felt a tap on the shoulder and heard a soft husky voice behind me saying, '*God dag, frøken! Hvordan står det til? Snakker De norsk?*'

I was travelling from Calais to Dover as a passenger aboard the *S.S. Halladale*, and I felt rather startled as I swung round to face a broad-shouldered sunburnt seaman who had high cheek-bones and triangular blue eyes. He surveyed me with an expression of humorous appraisal on his face.

'I'm afraid I didn't quite catch what you were saying,' I stammered.

'I am zo zorry,' he beamed, flashing me a smile of rugged brilliance. Then he explained that the Captain had mistaken me for a Scandinavian tourist, and had sent him along to ask if I would like to watch our approach to the white cliffs of Dover from the bridge.

'Tell the Captain I should be delighted to accept his invitation,' I replied, struggling hard to suppress an overwhelming desire to giggle. 'But unfortunately I don't come from Norway but from the top of those same white cliffs you've just mentioned.

I Join the Merchant Navy

In fact I'm a close neighbour of the Captain's although I've never had the pleasure of meeting him before!'

I followed Narvik, as I later came to know him, along the crowded deck and up a steep ladder to the sacred precincts of the bridge; and there I came face to face with Captain John Eric Dawson, Master of the cross-Channel steamer, *S.S. Halladale*. It was the type of encounter which triggered off a number of lightning impressions, and the following thoughts flashed through my mind in quick succession . . .

'Master under God they call them . . . well this one certainly looks the part . . . obviously has a sense of humour . . . gets on well with all types of people . . . would hate a land job . . . must be really good in fogs, gales, collisions etc. . . . probably tiresome in fine weather . . . enjoys his food . . .'

At that point I became aware that the Captain was introducing me to everyone else on the bridge, inviting me to have a cup of coffee and pointing out the exact position of his home in St Margaret's Bay, all in the same breath. Then the Chief Officer showed me how the radar worked, and the quartermaster allowed me to hold the ship's wheel for a few magic seconds . . . The transition from deck to bridge had been so swift that I felt quite intoxicated with my surroundings on that lofty pinnacle so high above the common herd.

A few minutes later the signal station on the Eastern Arm in Dover hoisted the entry signal, and the *S.S. Halladale* steamed into the harbour with her Townsend house-flag flying out bravely in the fresh breeze: then she swung right round and moved slowly astern into her berth in the Camber. High above us the furrowed brow of the East Cliff mingled with the scurrying clouds, and the gulls came out of their holes to chatter and stretch their wings.

* * * * *

After our first meeting on the *S.S. Halladale*, I soon made friends with Jack Dawson and his wife and little boy who lived on the other side of the bay. They were a very cheerful and contented family, and I always enjoyed visiting their home and basking in the sunshine of their surroundings. I spent most weekends at Dolphin's Leap, a white house high up on the cliffs between the two lighthouses, and I was at home one winter's evening some three years after our first meeting, when Jack suddenly walked in and demanded: 'How would you like to become an assistant purser on our new ship for the summer season?'

I have never been good at making lightning decisions, so I havered and hesitated and put forward every sort of objection in order to gain time to think. 'I've had no training for anything like that,' I argued. 'And I've got a job in London anyway. Also I want to go for a short sailing holiday sometime this spring.'

He knew perfectly well that I was only trying to convince myself that the whole thing would be impossible out of contrariness, because I really wanted a job like that very badly.

'You don't need *any* training,' the Captain barked at me. 'Your three years at sea in the W.R.N.S. should have given you some idea of discipline and how an efficient ship's company is expected to run. The Head Purser, Muriel Chambers, is a qualified nurse which is the most important thing, and all you need is a great deal of tact and patience with which to handle the passengers, Head Purser and Captain! What languages can you speak?'

'French, German, Spanish, Serbo-Croat and a bit of...'

'That's enough!' he interrupted me. 'Well I don't see any reason to prevent you joining the ship on May 1st when we sign on the extra crew. You always told me that you loved the sea, and I don't suppose it would do you any harm to get away from London for a few months. Also you would still have time to fit in your sailing trip in April.'

He glared at me ferociously for a few seconds, then stood up to leave. 'I'll give you twenty-four hours to make up your mind..?'

Two minutes later the rear lights of his car glowed dimly on the rough track leading back to St Margaret's Bay.

* * * * *

Of course I said 'Yes', very early next morning. It was just the sort of job I had always longed to have and here was this glorious improbable chance, falling right into my lap. It was a

I Join the Merchant Navy

Sunday morning and the sun was sending intermittent beams of light through gaps in the heavy banks of cumulus clouds. A tanker filled the entire width of my sitting-room window, steaming majestically across the middle distance; and all the Dover seagulls were chuckling and shouting to one another above the chimney-pots. Suddenly I felt convinced that a new era was setting in, and I was determined not to miss any of the beautiful things it had to offer.

There had been some important changes in that smallest of all shipping companies, Townsend Ferries Ltd., since the fateful day when I crossed from Calais to Dover on the *S.S. Halladale*. The company had first been formed in 1928 by Captain Stuart Townsend, an ex-army officer who was a great pioneer in the early days of motoring. He was so upset by the rough treatment his car received during a Channel crossing aboard the mail steamer, that he suddenly decided to run a private car-ferry of his own! He started by chartering an ancient coaster which carried only fifteen cars and had no covered accommodation for the passengers; but, right from the beginning, she was such a success that Stuart Townsend soon purchased an old naval minesweeper for £5,000, and converted her into his first car-ferry, the *S.S. Forde*. Jack Dawson joined the *Forde* as Second Mate towards the end of her service on the cross-Channel run.

Soon after the Second World War the old minesweeper was replaced by the *S.S. Halladale*, a converted naval frigate which seemed quite palatial compared with Captain Townsend's previous vessels. He was not an ambitious businessman and never wanted to expand the company beyond his one car-ferry. Her crew were treated like part of his own family, and he was much loved by all who worked for him. Over the years a very happy atmosphere grew up in that tiny shipping company.

In 1957 Townsend Ferries became a public company. Captain Townsend was nearly seventy by then and felt compelled to make some provision for death duties. Half the shares were bought by a syndicate of Six Coventry businessmen, but it soon became apparent that the old Captain would never see eye to eye with them so, very reluctantly, he decided that it was time for him to retire. He had always visualized Townsend Ferries as remaining a one-ship company; but the men from Coventry had other ideas altogether and they promptly ordered a brand-new car-ferry of the very latest design to be built for them in Holland.

The first *Free Enterprise* was launched at Schiedam in 1962. Her hull was painted a delicate shade of lettuce-green and she had two red funnels, side by side, which rose defiantly above her lofty superstructure. She could carry 120 cars and 850 passengers, and was fitted with that brilliant new invention, a bow rudder, which made her easier to handle when moving astern into a narrow berth.

The *S.S. Halladale* was sold to Finland that summer, and Jack Dawson went over to Holland to take command of the new ship. The number of people wishing to cross to the Continent with their cars had increased to such an extent by then, that Townsend's were obliged to employ three crews during the summertime so that the *M.V. Free Enterprise* could continue running day and night for several months on end.

* * * * *

I returned to London the day after Captain Dawson's visit, and went straight to Gieves in Bond Street to order my new uniform. I was fairly bursting with self-importance when I stated my requirements to the man in 'uniforms' on the ground floor, but unfortunately he did not seem to share the sense of occasion which I felt the situation demanded.

'We only deal with gentlemen's uniforms on the ground floor,' he informed me rather pompously. 'If Madam cares to step upstairs to the Ladies' Department, I will send someone up there to measure her.'

I flew up the stairs, two at a time, and had a head-on collision in Ladies' Lingerie with a formidable personage in black crêpe-de-Chine who turned out to be the doyenne of all the shop assistants. She glared at me unpleasantly and ushered me into the nearest cubicle. All went well until the tailor threw me right off balance by enquiring in a stern tone of voice whether Madam wished to have the Cunard style of skirt, or the Wren officer's style? No one had mentioned this option to me before, and I

I Join the Merchant Navy

had no idea what the difference was between one style and the other; so I threw the ball back into his court and asked which one he personally would recommend. There was a long pause during which he looked me up and down with the eye of vast experience; at last a wintry smile briefly illuminated his face as he replied; 'In my opinion the Cunard skirt would suit Madam's type of figure to perfection.'

I was not sure whether he was being complimentary, or just plain rude; but as I had no immediate means of finding out, I agreed with his suggestion and ordered the Cunard skirt.

The following week-end I spoke to Captain Dawson on the telephone and told him about my uniform, but when I mentioned the Cunard skirt he seemed rather vague and reticent. 'You'd better ask Muriel about it next week,' he mumbled. 'And I'll give you a lift into Dover on Saturday morning, right?'

Muriel Chambers, the Head Purser, had suggested that I should cross to France and back with her one day before the summer season started, to learn what my job would involve and also, no doubt, so that she could judge if I was going to be any use to her or not.

The day trip over to Calais turned out to be a great success, and I knew that I should like working with Muriel the moment I saw her. She had started her life at sea as a stewardess aboard the *S.S. Halladale*, but she was so hard-working and conscientious that she was soon promoted to become the aged purser's assistant; and, when he retired, she was appointed Head Purser, the only woman Head Purser in the Merchant Navy at that time.

I learnt a good deal about the duties of an assistant purser that day, and met many of the crew as well as the French employees of Townsend's over in Calais. After disembarking our outward-bound cargo, we had ten minutes to spare for lunch before the loading would begin for the return voyage. Muriel was swallowing some rather hot Scotch broth when I asked her if she was wearing a Cunard skirt. I noticed a reddish flush spreading upwards from her neck, and her eyes began to bulge with the pain of the scalding soup going down too fast: 'Cunard skirt? Certainly not!' she snapped. 'This is the Wren officer's style of skirt with the two pleats in front to give it a flared effect. The Townsend pursers have *always* worn this style.'

A thought flashed through my mind that all the pursers had been men before Muriel appeared on the scene; but I thought it might be unwise to pursue that line of reasoning, so I dived straight in at the deep end, so to speak, and told her that I had already ordered a Cunard skirt. I shall never know what her reply would have been for the Good Lord arranged for the quartermaster to make an announcement over the loud-speaker just then, calling the purser down to the car-deck as the new passengers were beginning to come aboard.

Neither Muriel nor I alluded to the prickly subject of the Cunard skirt again, but as I turned to leave the office at the end of the day she called after me; 'Mind you show up in good time when we sign on the new crew on May 1st!'

* * * * *

I joined the Merchant Navy on a brilliant, cold, green morning, with a mighty wind blowing straight down the North Sea from its birthplace up in the Arctic Circle. The long thin sandbanks —Galloper, the North and South Falls, Sandettie, the Outer Ruytingen—were baring their treacherous spines as the green combers broke across them in clouds of foam and spindrift; and the sky above was apple-green, as clear and hard as a sheet of glass.

I caught an early bus into Dover that morning to make sure of reaching the *Free Enterprise* in plenty of time to change into my new uniform, as the signing on ceremony was due to start at nine o'clock.

'The important thing is to make a good first impression on people, no matter who they may be,' my father had counselled me when I was a child, and his advice flitted through my memory while I knotted my tie with nervous twitching fingers, then climbed into my tight-fitting Cunard skirt.

In due course I made my way up to the lounge-deck attired as a brand-new assistant purser and feeling desperately self-conscious, as I was convinced that all eyes would be fixed upon me. It came as something of a disappointment to discover that

I Join the Merchant Navy

no one had, apparently, even noticed my début as they were all too busy filling in forms, asking questions, demanding attention or just chatting with one another about this and that. There were more than a hundred crew members to be signed on, some of them old hands who returned to Dover year after year for the summer season.

Among the veteran sailors on the far side of the room I noticed a man with a rugged sunburnt complexion and eyes as blue as the Indian Ocean peering out from under a pair of fierce shaggy eyebrows. He looked as if he was a vital part of the wooden walls of England, the perfect image of a true British sea-dog; and yet he spoke with a quiet educated voice and behaved more like an ambassador than a traditional Merchant Navy mate.

Snowy, one of the older seamen who had just returned from a cruise to the South Pacific, whispered in my ear; 'That's the Ancient Mariner over there. He's got a mate's ticket in square-rig and they say he's been round Cape Horn umpteen times in a 4-masted barque. There's not many people left with square-rig tickets nowadays, I can tell you.'

'What's his real name?' I asked.

'I don't believe he's got one! He's always known as the A.M. aboard this ship and I doubt if he'd recognize himself by any other name.'

Snowy, himself, was square-built and strong, with mild blue eyes under a thatch of pure white hair which had earned him his nickname. While he was telling me about the A.M. he fixed me with a level gaze which was like the beam of a searchlight switched on to some dark object that had hitherto managed to remain anonymous.

The queue began to move forward and I realized that the signing on ceremony was about to commence. The most important man in the room appeared to be the Shipping Master, a solemn personage provided by the Department of Trade and Industry (Marine Division) to deal with all matters concerning the signing on or dismissing of any member of the crew. Muriel Chambers sat behind an adjacent desk, looking very spruce and businesslike. She was wearing her official face which was quite different from her everyday face. Next to her sat the man from the Merchant Navy Officer's Union, a dour individual of few words . . .

'Sign here,' he growled at me when I reached a position in front of his desk. There were no soft persuasive frills to make the business of being forced to join the Union more palatable.

At last the great moment had arrived and I found myself leaning over the Shipping Master's desk to sign the Ship's Articles. It was a moment of supreme significance, a vital landmark in my life; and whatever the outcome, I knew that I should never be quite the same again. The deed was done, and I moved away so that Snowy could take my place.

Presently I found myself on the top deck, just abaft the twin red funnels, with thousands of gulls shouting to each other below the East Cliff and the strong salty smell of the open sea borne in on the great north wind. Down below a long queue of cars was beginning to form on the far side of the custom-house, and out by the Eastern Arm big white horses were galloping across the olive-green sea. The quartermaster's voice suddenly announced that loading would commence in two minutes' time, so I turned and ran down several flights of stairs to the car-deck. The working day was about to begin.

* * * * *

The line of cars extended right across the assembly area, as far as the eye could see. It had split itself into the shape of a V, and the end of one prong advanced towards Muriel while the other one crept inexorably closer to me. The leading car was an ancient Daimler with four pairs of eyes focussed upon me, the near-side windows having been wound down to give the occupants an unimpeded view. I felt exposed and totally incompetent, and I began to wonder if I had sprung a ladder in my left stocking as I nervously demanded their tickets. The driver wore a loud check suit and motoring cap to match, and he addressed me as 'My good woman' which did nothing to dispel my gloomy forebodings.

My next car was a battered Hillman Hunter containing a laughing family of Cockneys. The father leant out of his window and said; 'Cheer up, luv; we ain't goin' ter eat yer!'

I felt better after that, and ready to face whatever the car-park attendant or fate had next to offer me. It turned out to be a flirtatious playboy type of person, the sole occupant of a magnificent silver-blue Maserati, a king among cars. He flashed me a warm brown look and suggested that I should jump in beside him and take a little 'promenade' down to St Tropez. The cars behind were becoming restive so I hastily seized his ticket and turned my attention to the next in line, a travel-worn coach called the Indiaman. That amazing old vehicle did a regular run from London to India every few weeks, carrying parties of students and travellers who paid very little for their fares and were prepared to sleep, cook and live aboard the coach for days on end.

For another half hour or so they kept on coming . . . little Morris 1,000s, powerful Mercedes, Lancias and Alfa-Romeos, Fords and a marvellous Bugatti driven by a tall blond man with the light of adventure in his eyes.

At last there were no more cars left in the assembly area and Mr Briggs, an ambitious Scottish clerk from Townsend's office, strolled across to tell Muriel that he had no one left on the other side of the custom-house. We ran down the ramp and on to the car-deck, and a moment later a piercing whistle sounded somewhere above my head; simultaneously the great stern door began to shut with a deep rumbling noise, like the sudden closure of Aladdin's Cave. I could feel the engines throbbing beneath the iron deck on which I stood, and up above there were heavy rope hawsers being pulled through fairleads, orders being shouted and men's boots tramping to and fro on the after deck. It was all quite marvellous, for I knew by then that we were under way.

Five miles out from Dover any remote comfort a vessel might derive from being under the lee of the North Foreland is soon lost in a strong north-easterly wind. Fortunately I could not actually see the sea from the purser's office, but its boisterous tendencies that morning were faithfully reflected on the faces of the hardy motorists who had ventured to cross the Channel so early in the season.

Muriel's mood was brisk and cheerful, and she passed me a large handful of tickets to count and a few forms to fill in on the optimistic assumption that I had remembered some of the things she had taught me during that previous voyage, which seemed like a thousand years ago. I tried to concentrate with all my will-power, but the chair on which I sat moved up and down with a shuddering jar from time to time, and the soles of my feet tingled with strange vibrations; and various objects on our desk such as the ink-well, a tray full of pens and pencils and a franking machine seemed to be charged with a separate life of their own.

Presently I became aware of an angry red face, punctuated by a pair of fierce brown eyes, a flattish nose with flaring nostrils and a straight trap of a mouth, only a few inches away from my own. Startled out of any further reflections on the delicate state of my inside, I stared nervously back then looked to Muriel for assistance, but she was standing outside the office talking to Eric Bradwell, the Head Steward. The trap opened to reveal some decayed brown incisors, and a noise escaped from it which made me think of a bear awaking after its long winter hibernation.

'I'm goin' ter soo your lousy company fer what's 'appened ter my rabbits!' he roared at me. 'Whatcher goin' ter do abaht them, Mrs Bloody Purser?'

'I haven't touched your rabbits!' I shouted back in some alarm. 'I didn't even know you'd brought any aboard.'

'I've got twendy-fower Chinchilla bucks in me caravan, and 'alf of 'em's frown up their dinners what I give 'em in Dover and the uvver 'alf's fainted! Nah, whatcher got ter say?'

His angry brown eyes were beginning to hypnotize me and I felt like a cornered rabbit myself, completely bereft of the valuable power of speech. Muriel, who was used to dealing with all types of passengers, had come back into the office and sized up the situation in a few seconds. She pushed me to one side and stared him straight back in the eye-balls.

'What d'you mean by coming aboard with all those rabbits without a permit?' she rushed into the offensive. 'I shall have to ask the Radio Officer to send through a signal to the French customs before we dock in Calais. If you ever travel this way again, *all* livestock must be reported to the Head Purser the moment you board the ship, understand? Also *no* passengers are allowed on the car-deck while we are at sea, under any circumstances.'

I Join the Merchant Navy 141

Muriel sat down and started to fill in the cargo manifest to indicate that the interview was over. The rabbit man suddenly looked quite ordinary and deflated, all the wind having been shaken out of his sails. He had no idea whether rabbits were allowed into France or not, but as he had no means of finding out until he landed there, an expression of confusion and anxiety settled on his florid brow. As soon as he was out of sight Muriel heaved a big sigh of relief, ordered two cups of coffee from the snack-bar and exclaimed; 'You name them we get them!'

The next occurrence on the first voyage from Dover to Calais was Captain's rounds. Jack Dawson never came into a room without being noticed, for that was not his nature. He arrived like an irrepressible whirlwind, full of splendid new ideas and optimistic plans; invariably he caused a mighty unheaval of all the papers on our desk and left behind him a trail of sun-glasses, navigational instruments and ship's papers which were rounded up by the duty quartermaster or Paddy Powers, his Irish steward, after his passage across the lounge-deck.

'Isn't it cold and windy up on the bridge this morning?' I asked him with the simplicity of a complete novice.

'Good gracious, no!' he bellowed with laughter. 'Mr Boys has turned the central heating on full blast and it's as warm and cosy as an igloo! It wasn't like that when I first went to sea, mind you,' he continued, the light of reminiscence twinkling in his eyes. 'I joined a tramp steamer called the *Orange River* carrying coal across the Atlantic to South America, and one of my first jobs as a boy was to trim the wicks of all the oil lamps aboard. In those days the Master and officers kept watch on an open bridge in all types of weather, and it was considered completely irresponsible and quite out of the question to spend any part of one's duty watch under cover.'

The Captain swept on into the snack-bar, for he made a point of paying a visit to all the departments in the ship each morning.

'Just to make sure that everyone's on the ball and happy at their jobs,' he told people who expressed an interest in the matter. 'Also it's important for the crew to see me as well as me seeing them, so that they don't think I'm just a stuffed dummy sitting up there on the bridge!'

Time passed very quickly on the short Channel crossing and Paddy looked in to tell us that we were passing the whistle buoy on the Riden de Calais soon after Captain's rounds that morning. Muriel said she wanted to have a word with the Radio Officer, and asked me to hold the fort for a few minutes while she was away.

Suddenly I was there alone, in charge of all sorts of secret documents and vast sums of money, and feeling as proud as a prize peacock. I sat on my throne in that tiny office and surveyed the lesser mortals on the lounge-deck with a smirk of condescension on my face. A small boy stood on tiptoe to bring his eyes level with the top of my counter, and enquired in a squeaky little voice; 'Please, Miss, do you sell comics here?'

Before I had time to reply, a brusque figure wearing the uniform of a petty officer swept the child to one side and, planting both elbows squarely on the counter, he fixed me with an investigatory stare.

'Who are you?' he demanded in a truculent tone.

'The new assistant purser,' I mumbled, feeling rather deflated and less important than I had done before his arrival. I stared straight back at him and decided he was what my mother would describe as a *beau garçon*.

'Well I'm Charlie Walker, the Bos'un,' he announced loftily. 'And if you do exactly what I tell you, you won't go far wrong, my girl!'

'I thought I was meant to come under Muriel's department?' I felt trapped and on the defensive.

'ALL departments come under Charlie Walker, including a few of the passengers as well!' One of his eyelids descended briefly, obscuring a very sharp grey eye, and he emitted a bellow of laughter which caused the whole office to vibrate.

The voice of the quartermaster announcing 'Harbour Stations, Harbour Stations... Stand by fore and aft' came over the loudspeaker system at that moment, and Charlie Walker vanished from sight. Simultaneously Muriel reappeared and invited me to come down to the car-deck to help her collect the landing-tickets.

We waited close to the big stern door while the ship manoeuvred slowly into her berth. A greaser was standing by to switch on the hydraulic mechanism for opening the door, and the duty engineer waited on the other side of the entrance in case any hitches should occur. As soon as it was open the cars began to move forward, and each one paused beside the purser for its occupants to give up their landing-tickets, then drove off the ship into France.

Muriel had put me in charge of the Calais Bag, a magic satchel which often contained not only the ship's papers for the French office, but a variety of other items such as legs of Canterbury lamb and Marks and Spencer cardigans, et cetera. She and I walked up the ramp behind the last car, and five or six men from the Calais mooring-party, clad in delphinium-blue dungarees, advanced to meet us with broad smiles of welcome on their faces. They all shook hands with Muriel and me and enquired politely after the state of our health; then Muriel led me into the custom-house where we were greeted effusively by a tall dark policeman called Pierrot, who introduced us to his *copain*, Raphael. Then a charming old gentleman, with white hair partially concealed beneath a brown trilby hat, came out of a small office and presented Muriel with a large bouquet of red carnations. Afterwards I discovered that she had brought over something rather special for his Sunday dinner in the Calais Bag, and this was his way of thanking her.

Muriel followed old Billy Steer into the R.A.C. office, and left me at the entrance to the custom-house with instructions to intercept any early motorists for the return passage.

'I hope that you are able to converse in the French tongue?' Pierrot was towering over me like some immense Latin question-mark, a stern, almost saturnine, expression flickering around the corners of his mouth. I noticed that he looked totally and irresistably French, with a hint of sadness lurking in the depths of those very brown eyes. He went on to tell me that none of the other pursers could understand more than a couple of words in French, and he was looking forward to having some *petites causettes* with me while awaiting the arrival of the passengers. This disclosure gave me a pleasant sensation of superiority, and I had just launched into a few observations in my best French when two engineers from the *Free Enterprise* strode into the custom-house and called out to me; 'Don't believe a word those

Frogs tell you! They've all got one-track minds over here, once they start chatting up a bird!'

Pierrot did not seem to understand them, and I was so angry with their advice that I readily accepted his offer to bring me *une tranche de pâté maison* next time he was on duty.

The sea was no less boisterous on the return voyage from Calais to Dover; if anything the wind had hardened and the tide was now running against it, which transformed the whole seascape into a cauldron of hissing white-capped waves. It was no longer possible to open the doors on the windward side of the ship, and the few unhappy travellers on the lounge-deck sat huddled inside their overcoats, green-faced and introspective, ready to leap out on to the leeward deck at a moment's notice.

I found the task of filling in forms and manifests for the Dover Bag far more complicated than I had remembered. There were no less than sixteen forms to be completed and when the ship took a sudden swerve to port, causing me to fall off my chair and land in a crumpled heap on the floor of the office, I failed to perceive the slightest humour in my position. The Bos'un, who had looked in to see how we were getting on, was, however, convulsed with uncontrollable paroxysms of laughter; 'The A.M.'s in charge on the bridge right now,' he explained, with tears of mirth pouring down his cheeks. 'And he believes in sticking strictly to the Rule of the Road. If some bastard cuts across our bows when he ought to give way, we hold our course and speed up to the last possible minute, then the quartermaster shoves the wheel hard over and the A.M. rushes out to shake his fist and swear at the other ship as we scrape past her. Don't you worry, you're not the first one to land on your arse on the deck when we suddenly change course!'

During the course of the return voyage the whole ship's company came to our office to sign a form required by the British customs, and I noticed that Muriel knew a great deal about each man's family and background, and always found time to chat for a few minutes with each one in turn. She was immensely popular with everyone aboard, and I never heard an unkind word spoken about her by any member of the crew.

As the ship drew close to the harbour entrance, the pace of our work accelerated sharply. Jack Dawson had already looked

I Join the Merchant Navy

into the office several times to sign things and ask how I was getting on; then the cashier hung over us, waiting for his money and debit notes; simultaneously a dozen or more passengers thought of some vital last minute questions to ask; and the French passport officer, who had finished his work and found himself at a loose end, leant across our counter and said to Muriel; '*Bonjour, Madame Persaire!* 'Ow are you? *Je vois que vous avez une nouvelle assistante?*'

The procedure at the Dover end was quite different to Calais. After the *Free Enterprise* had berthed we were compelled to wait for the Customs to come aboard and clear the ship. Occasionally this took a long time if the rummage gang accompanied them and had a remunerative search among the crew's belongings. Following close on their heels came a representative from Townsend's office in the Eastern Docks, and he received the Dover Bag from Muriel and brought the latest gossip from the town. Finally Paddy came to our office bearing two glasses of some powerful concoction which he had christened 'Purser's pick-me-up'.

'That'll be after makin' you feel as happy as skylarks!' he predicted in his lilting Irish brogue.

He was right and it did, temporarily. But by the time we had disgorged one lot of passengers and started loading again for the next voyage to France, I felt ready to go to bed. It was only 4 p.m. and there were six more hours to get through before we should come off duty, but already the strain was beginning to tell. I struggled on through the next two crossings, trying desperately to prevent my eyelids from drooping and to appear alert and intelligent, when all I wanted to do was to put my head on the desk and fall asleep!

At last the long long day was over. Four Channel crossings, and a thousand new impressions whirling round in my throbbing head. We came ashore soon after ten o'clock, and Jack Dawson drove me back home. The wind had dropped and it was a clear cold night with the constellation of The Great Bear standing sentinel above the roof of my house, and the lighthouse on Cap Gris Nez winking at me in a friendly manner on the other side of the Dover Strait.

* * * * *

After a few days of catching the bus into Dover or accepting a lift in someone else's car, it soon became apparent that a car of my own would be a considerable asset. No sooner had the thought entered my head and been mooted aboard the ship, than a suitable little car of exactly the right price was discovered by the Captain at Henly's Garage in Dover. He was always like that; you had only to mention that you wished to travel to the moon, and he would find a satellite with a spare seat in it within a matter of hours.

Although I had driven a car for several years, I had never actually possessed one of my own before; so the arrival of *My First Car* was something of an event. It was an ancient Ford Popular costing exactly £100, and the day after its delivery the Captain instructed me to call at his home punctually at 9 a.m., as he planned to leave his own car behind and escort me into Dover until I was quite used to driving it. Accordingly I pulled up outside Robin Hatch on the dot of nine to find Jack Dawson running round his garden attempting to catch his Aberdeen terrier bitch, Chloë, before setting off to work.

'Never leave home till I see the ship on the horizon,' he panted at me, making a sweeping gesture towards France with one arm while he tried to grab Chloë's tail with the other. She scampered into the middle of a gorse bush, and I could see her bright eyes glowing with excitement as her master plunged in after her.

'A ship can't leave without its Captain,' I reflected, as I crouched on the far side of the bush and tried to cut off Chloë's retreat. It is hard to estimate how long we might have spent rounding up the nimble terrier if little Simon Dawson had not emerged from the house just then, and lured her out of the bush by holding a ginger biscuit close to her black furry face.

The *Free Enterprise* had been *on* the horizon some minutes ago, and was emphatically *off* it by the time we had bundled ourselves into the car and set off at a hair-raising speed—with the Captain at the helm—to collect Bill Barnett, the Mate, from the caravan site at Martin Mill. Then we flew across the hills to River to fetch Eveline Hover, the stewardess; dropped Simon at his school, and finally picked up Dapper, a free-and-easy Geordie seaman who showed every sign of being even later than

I Join the Merchant Navy

his skipper when we intercepted him sauntering across the Market Square. At one minute to ten we merged with the rest of the crew who were waiting at the top of the ramp to board the ship as soon as she had been cleared by the Customs.

Those pre-work encounters with the whole of A Watch were something of an experience in the early days. Everyone wore civilian clothes and suddenly they appeared as individuals and strangers, instead of the hard-working, lazy, tragic, funny, disagreeable or lovable members of the same big family into which I was gradually becoming assimilated. Some of them looked shy and unprotected, others stylish and over-confident, and a few just looked themselves.

Presently B Watch came trooping up the ramp, their white faces and red-rimmed eyes proclaiming that they had had a rough night at sea. They carried three-foot-long French loaves tucked under their arms and several hours' growth of stubble on their chins. For a few moments the two watches mingled together, a heterogeneous crowd of men and women who shared a common bond in that each one of them was a vital and immensely important part of that most wonderful of all God's creations, a happy and efficient ship's company.

During the early part of May our watch was on 'days', which meant that we worked for twelve hours, from 10 a.m. until 10 p.m., two days running, then had one full day off duty. I soon grew accustomed to the four voyages in one day, and by the end of the first week I no longer felt worn out after twelve hours on duty. The ship was seldom more than half full as the real holiday season had not yet begun; because of this we usually had time to spend at least ten minutes over our meals in the dining-saloon, to run up to the top deck and take great gulps of pure salt air from time to time, and to chat with some of the passengers and pay fleeting visits to other departments on the ship, where there was often a cup of tea or glass of beer waiting for us. But all too soon the quartermaster's voice would come thundering over the loudspeaker; 'Harbour Stations, Harbour Stations . . . Stand by fore and aft.'

* * * *

Mr Foster, the Second Mate, was a thin pale-faced young man who took his profession very seriously. He was not the sort of person one would ever dream of associating with flirtatious overtures or similar frivolities, but he was able to explain to me the causes of sea fog in a very scientific manner on the day that we found ourselves crossing the Dover Strait in a thick pea-souper. There were only a few passengers that day and most of them sat huddled on the upper deck with their coat collars pulled up round their ears, ice-cold droplets forming at the ends of their noses and expressions of uncertainty and alarm haunting their straining eyes.

Patrick Quinn, the Radio Officer, looked in to tell us that the fog was growing thicker, and also to announce his intention of getting married in a few days' time! He was a man of a certain age with grey wavy hair, an engaging smile and a profound interest in his own medical symptoms which he often liked to discuss with Muriel and me. But on that particular day Patrick was quite carried away by the bold decision he had made the previous night. Helen, his intended bride, had been introduced to him by Captain Dawson when she was crossing to France on the *Free Enterprise* earlier that spring. To everyone's astonishment she elected to spend the entire passage in the Radio Office, even though the sun was shining warmly on the upper deck and light refreshments were being served in the Captain's cabin. And a few weeks later, in the middle of that impenetrable fog, Muriel ordered three glasses of vodka and lime from the bar so that we could drink to the future happiness of Patrick and his fiancée.

Presently Tubby Groves, the quartermaster who resembled the full moon, came down from the bridge and strolled across to have a word with us. When Muriel remarked that he must have had a difficult watch up there, he replied feelingly; 'It doesn't matter how thick it gets with the Old Man on the bridge. He's a bloody marvel in weather like this!'

It grew thicker every hour, and during the last voyage back from Calais you could hardly see one end of the ship from the other. Jack Dawson had never left the bridge that day; there were no Captain's rounds or pleasant little chats with the passengers, or a quiet hour devoted to the ship's correspondence.

I Join the Merchant Navy

This was the real thing, the time when he came into his own; and every single person aboard that ship was depending on his skill and judgement to bring them safely home.

About 11 p.m., after thirteen hours on duty, we slid quietly into our berth on the west side of the Camber, but it was not until our mooring lines were secured that I was able to make out the ghostly outline of the concrete jetty.

'That's what they mean by "Master under God",' Snowy informed me, as we waited together on the car-deck for the stern door to open.

* * * * *

During Captain's rounds next morning Jack told us about a new order which had just been issued by the Department of Trade and Industry. Every merchant ship, it announced, must carry a specified number of certificated lifeboatmen, and more crew members must be trained if there were not already enough in the ship's company. There had been a terrible disaster the previous winter when the Greek cruising-ship, *S.S. Lakonia*, sank near the Canary Islands and, despite the calmness of the sea, many of the passengers and crew had inexplicably lost their lives.

As a result of this order a number of us found ourselves studying the various facets of lifeboatmanship in all our spare moments during the next few weeks. Altogether there were about fifteen of us on A Watch; mainly stewards, shop-girls, Eveline, the stewardess, and two or three new seamen. Mr Foster gave us instruction in the rudiments of pilotage, coastal navigation and meteorology; but the practical side of lowering a ship's lifeboat and handling it under way was left to Charlie Walker, the Bos'un, to teach us.

Every afternoon on our return from the first voyage to Calais, a holiday atmosphere prevailed on the boat-deck for a short while. No sooner had the last car driven off the ship than the budding lifeboatmen appeared on deck attired in an odd assortment of dungarees, bright-coloured slacks, and ancient shirts or blouses. The older seamen, who had been through it all themselves, clustered round us to watch the fun. First of all we had to prepare, swing out and lower the lifeboat, at the same time keeping it clear of the ship's side. Charlie bawled instructions at each of us in turn, and woe betide anyone who released the gripes too soon or wound the crank handles on the davits faster at one end of the boat than the other. Once afloat in the Camber, Charlie's patter was like the staccato firing of a machine-gun:

'Ship the tiller, Number 10 . . . Hard over to starboard . . . You up there in the bows, let go the ruddy toggle . . . Pass the painter along the inboard side you set of lily-livered landlubbers . . . Toss oars . . . Let go for'ard and bear off, Number Bloody One . . . Down oars . . . Ship your crutches . . . What'cher mean, don't know what a crutch is? I'll soon show you when we get back aboard! . . . *Give Way together* you load of half-baked toad's spawn . . . None of that feathering lark in a ship's lifeboat, Number 5; you're out on the open sea a thousand miles from land, and not on the effing Serpentine . . . Show us how you'd step the mast, Number 4 . . . What's the garboard strake, Number 2? . . . What you've just done's called catching a crab, you silly puking idiot . . .'

He seldom drew breath during the whole period of instruction, and the timbre of his voice was such that I often noticed rows of astonished spectators lining the decks of one of the French or Belgian car-ferries, waiting for her signal to leave harbour.

* * * * *

I started night duty for the first time on June 13th. It was a quiet dark night without a star in the sky, and only a handful of motorists and three caravans on the first trip from Dover to Calais. Muriel and I received our small quota of passengers at the top of the ramp during the magic hour of twilight, and straightaway we seemed to have stepped into another world. Usually our first loading was packed with incidents; the group of day-trippers who try to sidle aboard without passports or identity-cards; an extra coach to be squeezed on to the overcrowded car-deck at the last minute; neurotic messages from the Dover office about some unexpected V.I.P.s, to be handled with great charm and discretion. But that June evening was very quiet and peaceful, and as soon as the cars and caravans were safely parked on the car-deck, Muriel and I had nothing more to do until the ship left harbour.

I Join the Merchant Navy

We chatted with Ernest, an elderly car-park attendant who had some interesting views on human psychology; then little Friz, the sixteen year old deck-boy, came over to join us and told me about his pet rabbits and the sort of things they liked to eat. He had a thin sensitive face and clear brown eyes which radiated beams of purest innocence, and a tendency to blush very easily when spoken to. But, despite appearances to the contrary, he was a dedicated and single-minded seaman from the top of his sailor's cap to the soles of his tough black seaboots.

The East Cliff loomed above us in dim mysterious grandeur, as tall and aloof as the mountains of the moon, and the urgent siren of an outward bound ship rent the night air somewhere over on the far side of the harbour. Suddenly I felt an overwhelming surge of excitement as I stood there under the huge black arc of the heavens; it seemed quite wonderful just to be alive.

The spacious pattern of our routine jobs at the loading ramp was continued in the purser's office, as the counting of tickets and filling in of forms for the Calais Bag took no more than fifteen or twenty minutes. Landing in Calais at midnight we found Pierrot and Raphael on duty in the custom-house, and because there were only five cars booked for the return passage to Dover we had plenty of time to talk.

'Why do you English converse mainly about the weather, the price of meat or the places you have visited on the Continent?' asked the tall Frenchman. 'Here in France one likes to discuss subjects of personal interest, the things which are closest to the heart, you understand? For instance, if I should ask, "Have you ever been married? Was your husband faithful to you? Why are your eyes so sad? Do you sleep with many different men? Tell me the most beautiful experience of your life . . . ?" You would desire, perhaps, not to answer these questions on account of the famous British reserve, *n'est-ce-pas*?'

'It is possible!' I agreed. 'We seldom talk about the subjects of deepest importance to us. Most Europeans think that we are hypocrites, but perhaps we do not want the most intimate details of our lives exposed to the general public.'

'Surely you would not class me as the general public?' demanded Pierrot, with a hurt expression in his eyes.

I was saved from further complications by the arrival of our first vehicle, a mini-van filled with Laplanders who wore reindeerskin driving-jackets. The fourth car had C.D. plates prominently displayed, and it contained a Mr Popović and one other gentleman from Belgrade, heading for the Jugoslav Embassy in London.

'*Zdravo!*' exclaimed the dashing diplomat, as he wound down the window of his ancient Fiat and flashed me a smile of disarming radiance. 'You are exactly my first experienze of Engleska!'

I received his ticket with a warm glow of pleasure, as I could not remember ever having been anyone's first experience of anything before. Then I glanced at Pierrot, and the black thunder-cloud type of expression on his face made me realize that Mr Popović was, after all, only a transient passenger, a ship that passes in the night, and definitely *not* to be considered as one of us.

The *Free Enterprise* left Calais at 1 a.m., and when I returned to the purser's office Muriel told me to go to bed for an hour or two as she would attend to our next arrival and reloading in Dover. When the nights were quiet with only a few people travelling, she explained, we could divide our work on the second and third crossings, and each have a chance to sleep for a short while; but we should always work together in the office on the first and last crossings when there were more jobs to be done and the Captain was prowling round the ship.

* * * * *

'... will all passengers please rejoin their cars now.'

I awoke with a start, wondering where on earth I was; then it gradually dawned on me that we had crossed the Channel twice since I fell asleep, and were now about to dock in Calais for the second time that night. I leapt into my skirt and jacket and ran back to the office, suffering from severe qualms of conscience. But Muriel greeted me with a cheerful smile and said she had looked into the cabin in Dover, but I was sleeping so soundly that it had seemed a pity to wake me as there was very little work to do. She asked me to take the Calais Bag ashore for her and look after the last loading back to Dover.

I Join the Merchant Navy   153

It was 5.30 a.m. and the French seaport was bathed in the gentle grey light of dawn. The Calais mooring-party advanced to meet me as I strode importantly up the ramp in sole charge of that magic leather satchel, and we all shook hands and enquired after the condition of each other's health in a manner which completely concealed from the British motorists the fact that we had only parted at 1 a.m. that same morning!

The inside of the custom-house was filled with the rustlings and twitterings of small birds waking up among the rafters, and the occasional cooing of some sleepy French pigeon which was perched on top of the sloping roof. Another pair of policemen, Yves and Léon, had taken the place of Pierrot and Raphael, and they were arguing fiercely with three or four British drunks who, having missed their return passages on the *Queen of the Channel* the previous night, had climbed over the fence with a view to sidling aboard the *Free Enterprise* unobserved. As I hurried past them I heard Yves suggesting to his mate that they relieve themselves of this *ordures* by cramming it down the main drainage system in Calais.

I took the bag into the Townsend office, and spent a few minutes chatting with old Billy Steer and Monsieur Delanghe, *un homme très sérieux*, who was the French manager. Presently I set off on a short walk round the docks, as the loading for the return voyage was not due to start before 6.15 a.m. I wandered round the edge of the Bassin Carnot, where the Scandinavian and Russian freighters discharged their cargoes of timber. There was no one about and the sleeping ships floated placidly under the soft grey sky. Half way round the Bassin I came to a mound of pine logs which were still damp from the previous night's dew and their scent was strong and pungent, reminding me of the great pine forests of Finland and my voyage there in *Martha*. I sat down on the edge of the mound and drifted into a beautiful daydream in which a famous orchestra was playing Sibelius' Fourth Symphony on the poop-deck of the ship moored a few yards further along the quay. Then a clock struck six in the centre of the town, and I awoke from my dream and hurried back to the Gare Maritime and the next loading for Dover.

The last voyage was very calm and peaceful. Muriel and I each had time for a substantial breakfast in the dining-saloon, then we filled in the last set of papers for Dover and received a visit from Patrick Quinn; he gave us the latest meteorological details to enter on to our weather form, and also told us a few hair-raising details about the present state of his kidneys. He was now a married man, and the weight of his marital responsibilities seemed to be having a depressing effect on his constitution.

Finally, there was just time for a glass of rum with Charlie Walker in the Bos'un's quarters before the familiar sound of the quartermaster's voice came booming over the loud-speaker, calling all the seamen to harbour stations. And thus ended my first night at sea on the *Free Enterprise*.

* * * * *

During a period of night duties, which occurred every third week from the middle of June until the end of September, we worked an eighty-four-hour week which often extended itself into ninety hours or more when the ship was running late because of engine trouble or bad weather. This was not too hard in June as there was nearly always time to snatch an hour or two of sleep; but during the months of July and August we were both working all night long, except on a few rare occasions in mid-week, and it became much harder to sleep during the hot summer days at home. However, my first week of nights was an easy and gentle introduction as the weather was fine, the sea calm and the moon growing bigger and bigger every night.

We could not continue our lifeboat drill that week, but I spent all my spare moments in the office revising the theory of simple navigation. Our exam was due to take place in a week's time, so I usually slept with the book under my pillow in the daytime as well. Sometimes I lay down among the wild flowers near the old lighthouse when I came off duty; there was a marvellous crop of cowslips, forget-me-nots, buttercups and daisies growing in thick clusters all over the grass that summer, and some mornings I could hear a blackbird singing its heart out in the upper branches of an evergreen oak. My dog hunted for rabbits on the edge of the cliffs and the bees buzzed contentedly among the flowering shrubs, while pure white gulls soared in the blue heavens above me. It was quite idyllic out

I Join the Merchant Navy

there, but I never managed to sleep for more than an hour or two. Then there was *Martha*, calling out for some urgent attention in Dover; and the lifeboat examination looming over me like a black cloud. So what with one thing and another, I began to feel a bit lethargic by the end of the week.

During our last night on duty I ran out on deck for a breath of fresh air just as we were coming into Calais Harbour. It was low water and the pungent smell of French mud, stale fish, garlic and Gaulloise tobacco was all around me. I had grown to love that smell during the past month, and I felt very contented that night as I inhaled deeply before running down to the car-deck to collect the landing-tickets.

* * * * *

The Lifeboat Certificate first came into being as a result of investigations made into the sinking of the *Titanic* in 1912. The Court of Inquiry recommended, among other things, that 'in cases where the deck-hands are not sufficient to man the boats, enough other members of the crew should be trained in boat work to make up the deficiency. These men should be required to pass a test in boat work.'

I arrived at the Wellington Dock on the morning of our examination wearing my smartest sailing outfit. All the others were there already; the stewards and shop-girls and Eveline and the seamen who were not already qualified lifeboatmen.

'I'd like you to start by boxing the compass from south-west by south round to east by north,' said the man from the Ministry of Transport, fixing me with a penetrating stare.

'Vile pig!' I thought to myself. 'Fancy picking on me to box the rotten thing backwards before we've hardly started!'

But all those quiet nights in the Purser's Office and sunny days in the garden had borne their fruit, and I believe that I could have boxed a compass standing on my head if he had asked me to do so.

'Describe the contents of the first aid kit, as specified by the Ministry of Transport,' he snapped at Eveline, who was watching a man scaling a tall mast on the far side of the dock. She was dressed in smart navy-blue trousers and a pink crocheted blouse, and he had no means of knowing that the first aid kit was something with which she was all too familiar.

After those first two questions the examiner softened visibly, and by the time we had struggled through the technical details of a lifeboat's construction, the entire launching procedure, the use of an oil bag in a rough sea, the contents of the Distress Signal Kit and the method of recovering our sea anchor, he was positively beaming. This was just as well, for the next part of the examination, which involved the handling of a lifeboat in a fresh breeze under oars and sail, left much to be desired.

One of the stewards started the downward trend by catching a crab as soon as we had pulled away from the quay. Some of us were having difficulty in stifling our titters until we noticed the glacier-blue light which had crept into the examiner's eyes; the next moment he started firing orders at us without mercy. Each person had to take on the responsibilities of coxswain in turn, and during my spell in charge of the boat he told me to bring her alongside a fishing-vessel and to give all the appropriate commands to my crew. Happily oblivious of the strength and direction of the wind, we came sailing in rather splendidly under a press of canvas with all oars pulling lustily and a good Force 5 behind us. Our boat bore down upon her target at an exhilarating speed but, by some devious forethought, I had placed our brawniest mariner in the bows, and he was able to break the impact of our arrival with his strong muscular arms and also prevent the lifeboat from slicing a neighbouring dinghy in half.

The man from the Ministry of Transport turned to me with a wintry smile which did nothing to defrost the expression in his eyes, and observed; 'It is customary to turn a boat up into the wind before coming alongside another one, especially under sail.'

I felt unutterably foolish and chastened for I was, after all, one of the few in our group who had been fortunate enough to spend several years bringing sailing-boats up into the wind.

'That's the end of my Lifeboatman's Certificate,' I whispered miserably to Jonesy, one of my best friends among the stewards.

Perhaps the patient examiner read my thoughts, for he asked me several easy questions in quick succession which I was able to answer without disgracing myself any further, then he bade us all goodbye and said he was very pleased with our ability to handle a lifeboat. We looked at each other with astonishment, but a few days later Muriel received a sheaf of Lifeboatmen's Certificates from the Mercantile Marine Office, one of which, praise the Lord, bore my name.

The following afternoon there was a strong north-west wind blowing and the Captain experienced some difficulty in bringing the ship into her berth in Calais owing to the surge in the outer harbour, despite the fact that he was a pastmaster at docking in difficult conditions.

'With 9,000 tons underneath you, if you hit something you demolish it!' he told people who commented on his skill.

That afternoon in Calais he brought the ship to a halt a few yards farther away from the quay than usual on account of the wind and swell, and the seaman on the poop-deck had a hard job throwing the heaving-line far enough to reach the shore. One of the Calais mooring-party leant forward to catch it and suddenly lost his balance owing to something slippery underneath his sea-boots. He fell into the harbour, and a moment later his head disappeared under the heaving oily surface of the water with the ship's propellers thrashing round only a short distance away from his body. A cry of despair went up from the rest of the mooring-party, and someone shouted that he could not swim. Obviously there was no time to lose and one of our quartermasters, Ben Ashton, and his friend, Reg Stedman, did not pause even for a second. They dived into the water, knowing full well that they might be crushed by the enormous steel bulk of the ship's hull as it lunged against the quayside in the swell. Between them they grabbed hold of the Frenchman, who had lost consciousness by then, and dragged him to a flimsy rope ladder which had hastily been lowered over the starboard quarter; and two minutes later they were hoisted to safety aboard the ship.

In due course all the Calais dock workers organized a collection to buy some special gifts for Ben and Reg, and they were presented with medals for bravery by the French Chamber of Commerce. The whole ship's company basked in their glory, and whenever we came in contact with men from the British Railway ships we comported ourselves with an air of pride and even superiority, for was it not our ship's company which had thrown up a pair of heroes in the hour of need?

11. FERRY ME TO FRANCE

When I returned to work after three days' leave—blissfully idle days of sleeping, eating and sailing *Martha*—I noticed that a number of changes had taken place aboard the *Free Enterprise*. Suddenly we had moved into the mid-summer period and there was never a crossing, neither day nor night, when the car-decks were not completely full and the lounge-deck permanently overcrowded. The number of tickets to count, questions to answer, people to find who had come aboard without paying their fares, and extra details to include on all the forms and manifests had increased proportionately. We seldom had enough time for a meal in the dining-saloon any longer; only a hasty snack and a cup of coffee brought to the office.

'Why we're not all in hospital suffering from chronic ulcers, I shall never understand!' observed Muriel pessimistically, casting a malevolent glance at the mound of tired-looking ham sandwiches which had been sitting on our desk for the past hour, waiting to be eaten.

Bill Barnett, the Mate, had left to go deep-sea again, and he had been replaced by a younger man who was new to the Townsend Ferry Service. Ian Perriam bore a certain marked resemblance to Shalimar's smart mate of the full-rigged clipper ship, *Serena*. He was tall and thin, without an ounce of spare flesh or prospects of future flabbiness. He had close-cropped brown hair, a lean and handsome face and a hard steely look in his grey eyes which suggested that it might be unwise to argue with his decisions or to cross his path in any other way.

During that first week in July the wind was boisterous and the sea very rough. We spent a trying few days protecting our quarters from some of the more unfortunate passengers who suddenly felt sea-sick and lurched across to ask us the way to the nearest lavatory, then discovered that they had left it too late! After one such incident, a steward had just finished cleaning the office floor with his mop and bucket of disinfectant when I looked up from my desk and noticed that I had come under the searching surveillance of a sharp-featured dowager type of person, seated on the opposite side of the lounge-deck. Presently she rose to her feet and advanced towards me wearing the purposeful expression of someone who had a mission to fulfil.

'I saw your mother last month on my way north to visit the Dougall-Willoughbys,' she announced in a penetrating voice. 'And she told me about this *extraordinary* job of yours! Tell me, my dear, how long are you proposing to continue with this pursering business?'

She made pursering sound like fornication, and I noticed that the pupils of her eyes merged with a beige and brown speckled sector, similar to a quail's egg. Suddenly my collar seemed too tight and I began to feel like a scarlet woman under her censorious gaze: then I caught the eye of my special friend, the Ancient Mariner, who was making 'I am steaming to your rescue' signals behind her back.

'Would you excuse me, Madam' he said in his most ambassadorial manner. 'But I have an urgent message for our purser who is required on the bridge *immediately*.'

He conveyed the impression that the bridge was, in all respects, as important as Buckingham Palace, and that there was no chance of delaying my summons by even a fraction of a second.

I scaled the steps, two at a time, up to the highest elevation on our ship; and a few minutes later I was hanging over one wing of the bridge watching the long green waves with their foaming white crests surging up on the port quarter, and pondering upon the infinite variety and exquisite beauty of my life at sea.

At the end of the first week we were back on night duty again, and I was working temporarily with Anne, another assistant purser, as Muriel had taken charge of B Watch.

I opened the notebook on my desk and studied the first page with deep concentration. It ran as follows . . .

'3.30 a.m.—Load ship

4.30 a.m.—Ship leaves Dover . . . Sell tickets to passengers without any . . . Count tickets and fill in ticket return forms . . . Complete three forms for Calais Bag.

6 a.m.—Collect landing-tickets . . . Take bag to Calais office.

6.45 a.m.—Wake Head Purser! Start loading . . .'

I had done it all enough times before, and there was really nothing to worry about apart from a few trifling aggravations which were to be expected at the height of the summer season. The ship was filled to her maximum capacity that night, and more people than usual had come aboard without their tickets. As a result I had to summon each one in turn over the loudspeaker, and this upset all the other passengers and the crew members who were trying to snatch a few minutes' sleep. Also the French passport officer was behaving in a tiresome manner, perhaps on account of the disagreeable pitching motion as we headed into a rising gale. I had sent a steward down to his cabin to wake him at the last possible moment when he was meant to be on duty in the passport office, but he flatly refused to rise from his bunk and thoroughly upset the poor boy, who came from a genteel background, by describing him as the offspring of a grande passion between a baboon and a wart-hog.

Added to those other problems it was undoubtedly the worst part of the night; those excruciating ice-cold hours before the dawn breaks when one longs, above all else, to be fast asleep in a warm soft bed. But my main trouble was the fact that I was feeling extremely depressed as I had heard no news of Dick since our return from that memorable week-end in Gravelines, and Brian had told me that he was unlikely to be coming south again that summer. This gloomy state of affairs was not improved by a conversation I had with one of the engineers, who was suffering from all the irritations of a mid-summer breakdown in the engine-room.

'They should never employ women aboard a ship in my

opinion,' he growled, glaring at me in a ferocious manner. 'They're bound to cause trouble or bad luck in the long run. I mean look what's happened to my engines this week!'

'I don't see in what way I'm to blame for that!' I protested.

'Well, perhaps not you personally; but you mark my words, no good will come out of letting a pack of females loose on this ship! Do you know what they're calling us in the Dover Stage now? The *M.S. Free Intercourse*!'

'I wish I'd stuck to my own little boat if you feel like that about us! I suppose you don't object to women on sailing-boats?' I enquired without much optimism.

'Ruddy yachtsmen!' his eyebrows formed a straight black line, like the approach of a thundery squall. 'They should all be exterminated. Fancy doing that sort of thing for pleasure! All they do is to send up distress flares or hang about in the middle of harbour entrances when a proper ship wants to get in. You've no idea how much trouble they cause the Merchant Navy or how many men doing a decent job of work have to risk their lives for that load of crap!'

I felt thoroughly upset and disillusioned, for I had always imagined that the big ship mariners must admire, and sometimes envy, the brave little boats crewed by their amateur sailors.

The engineers lived in another world to the deck department, and they shared very few tastes in common. In their lives there was none of the glamour of bringing a ship into harbour under the gaze of an admiring audience, or shooting the sun with a sextant at midday, or communing with the stars from a wing of the bridge on a fine night at sea. Instead their working hours were spent in the bowels of the ship toiling among hot, noisy and greasy machinery, often under the most trying conditions when there was a big sea running. But I noticed that they loved their engines very deeply, with a fierce protective love which would tolerate no criticism or interference. And when they stepped ashore they carried with them an air of proud defiance which announced their presence on land like the loom of a lighthouse on a dark night at sea.

Charlie Walker was another person who caused me a certain amount of irritation during our first week of nights in July. He had been born under the sign of Aries and my book of character studies said that natives of that sign were impatient, fussy, domineering, prone to violent passions, unable to tolerate contrary opinions, and many of them were totally devoid of tact . . .

'That description fits you to a T!' I told the Bos'un, reading out the paragraph in question and carefully suppressing any of the nicer traits which followed immediately afterwards. He had just burst into the office for the third time in the past hour to bark some orders at me, when I was desperately trying to finish off the stores list for F. C. Magnier, the Calais shipbroker.

'Well it's better than being a rotten little Scorpion with its tail swinging right and left giving underhand stings!' he roared with laughter and gave me a pat on the shoulders which nearly knocked me off my seat.

At that moment our new Mate, Ian Perriam, who was also a Scorpion, marched into the office and said, 'What are you two squabbling about? Hurry up and get that Calais Bag ready then we'll all go for a brisk walk round the Bassin Carnot when we get ashore.'

The last night of that week was the culmination of all the horrid nights which had preceded it. The wind was already gusting Force 8 as I drove into the car park; and when my hat suddenly blew off during the first loading, a nautically-minded passenger who fancied himself as a humorist observed that the Beaufort Scale would now be judged by the strength of wind required to shift a purser's hat!

The early part of the night passed in a blurred haze of misery as I felt sea-sick on the first crossing from Dover to Calais. Perhaps it was the sight of so many other victims crouching green-faced and hollow-eyed all over the lounge-deck; or the long-suffering stewards constantly rushing by with their smelly mops and buckets of disinfectant; or the poor little boy who cried bitterly because he had mislaid his one-eyed tiger, then tottered across to our office before finally relieving himself of his dinner. Whatever the cause, I found it harder than ever to concentrate and I glared enviously at Anne from time to time, for she was sitting there looking as unruffled and soignée as the Queen Mother, apparently oblivious of all the unpleasant episodes happening around us.

During the second loading in Dover, in the early hours of the following morning, I became involved in a nasty argument with the Bos'un and told him to mind his own business and stop interfering in every other department on the ship. He became speechless with rage, and was beginning to grind his teeth as I flounced past him up the gangway.

'You really shouldn't have spoken to Charlie like that, you know. I've never seen him so upset before!' Anne reprimanded me, during our next crossing from Dover to Calais.

When Ben Ashton came in to sign the custom's declaration he confirmed her rebuke with a vivid description of the atmosphere on the seamen's mess-deck. Finally Ian Perriam looked in and muttered something about having me put in irons next time I fouled up the Bos'un's temper in that monstrous way!

As soon as I had finished counting all the tickets and filling in the Third Schedule and the form entitled 'Clearance Outwards and Victualling Bill' for the Calais Bag, I went out on deck to inhale some fresh air in the hope that it might stop the throbbing sensation in my head. The dawn had just begun to break and the wind was blowing Force 9. The sea was painted in sombre tones of grey and mauve, heaping itself up into waves like ghostly mountains crowned with snowcapped summits which suddenly disintegrated into avalanches of thundering white foam. The ship fell with an awful shudder into bottomless holes in the sea, and I fancied that I could hear the propellers whirring round in mid-air as the stern lifted itself up towards the menacing black clouds which were racing across the dawn sky.

I no longer felt sea-sick; the whole seascape was too majestic to allow one time to reflect on the trivial functions of one's own stomach. All the same I was not sorry to return to the stuffy security of the purser's office.

Because it was the last crossing of our last night in the week, the atmosphere on the return voyage to Dover was comparatively cheerful. But I was left in no doubt at all that Charlie was definitely *not* on speaking terms with me.

At last the ship was safely secured in her berth in the Camber and A Watch staggered ashore. The Captain had no car with him that morning so I offered him a lift back to St Margaret's Bay in mine.

'After a night like last night, do you ever feel like swallowing the anchor and going to live somewhere miles away from the sea?' I asked him on the way home.

'No, never!' he chuckled happily. 'I've been at sea for thirty-five years now and I've no wish to be anything else other than a seafarer. And if I had my life over again, I'd do precisely the same thing!'

* * * * *

There were long golden sunbeams streaming through a narrow gap at the top of the curtains, and I lay on my back trying to count a hundred thousand iridescent atoms dancing up and down those brilliant shafts of light. After a few moments I stretched my arms luxuriously and looked at the clock.

'At least twenty minutes more in bed,' I murmured to little Bonzo, who was sitting bolt upright near the door making very obvious going-out-time gestures.

Suddenly the telephone began to ring on the table beside my bed and Bonzo opened his mouth and emitted a low savage growl.

I picked up the receiver and a familiar voice at the other end of the line asked how I was and announced that he had finished his job at Hitchin and had just arrived at St Margaret's Bay as a locum to Bobby Melhuish for two or three weeks, and he hoped that we should be able to meet again soon?

'That was Dick from Gravelines!' I told Bonzo in a dazed whisper after I had put down the receiver. He was not impressed with this revelation and raised his lips to exhibit two rows of sharp white teeth.

Before going to work that morning I ran down the hill to the old lighthouse and sat for a while in the middle of a carpet of harebells and meadow-sweet which grew with wild abandon all over the edge of the cliffs. A huge bumble-bee buzzed happily round the old rosemary bush and some snow-white gulls soared above me, their motionless wings outlined against the deep-blue sky.

Coming back to earth with a start, I ran to the car and drove at a reckless speed across the cliffs to Dover, but loading had already begun by the time I had parked and sprinted through the custom-house and across the wide assembly area to the ramp. As I flashed past one of the car-park attendants he suddenly burst into song: *Who were you with last night? Out in the pale moonlight* . . .

Muriel was back on A Watch again. Although she had just finished a hectic night on duty and was now proposing to work for a further twelve hours to bring the sequence of Head Purser's duties back into the right order, she did not seem at all put out by my late arrival.

It was Bastille Day over in France and after we had shaken hands with a very jovial-looking Calais mooring-party who showed signs of wishing to embrace us instead, I noticed Pierrot ambling across the assembly area with pinkish eyes and a rather unsteady gait.

'I took a little glass before your arrival!' he announced with a hiccup. 'Shall we see if we can dance *le Twist*?'

He gripped Muriel and me by one arm each and began to dance us towards the custom-house where we narrowly missed a head-on collision with Monsieur Delanghe who rather obviously had not, as yet, begun to celebrate the storming of the Bastille.

The next day was long and featureless, with a certain amount of unpleasant bickering between the engineers and the seamen. It all began when one of the main engines broke down in Calais after our first crossing.

'Ruddy grease-monkeys! Absolutely useless pack of land-lubbers they are. Pity we can't go back to the good old days of sail!' exclaimed the duty quartermaster, raising his voice to a suitable pitch so that it would carry along the engineer's corridor from the open door of the bridge.

'Ships would run a lot better in this day and age without any piddling seamen on them at all!' growled the Second Engineer, as he paused beside me on the car-deck to give vent to his abrasive temper. 'It's us who keep the ships running, whichever way you look at it; and I can tell you it's no help whatsoever to have those ignorant bastards up on the bridge mucking our engines about with their damnfool manoeuvring!'

I tried to steer a middle course as I had heard that sort of talk before; and I noticed that there were certain rare occasions when even the Captain and the Chief Engineer treated each other with a studied politeness which somehow did not ring quite true. During the next three voyages we limped backwards and forwards across the Channel on one engine, with a group of men working tirelessly down in the bowels of the ship; meanwhile the passengers, seamen and stewards made peevish remarks about the length of time it was taking to get from France to England, or vice versa. However, thanks to our hardworking engineers, both main engines were running normally again by the following day.

* * * * *

'Harbour Stations, Harbour Stations . . . Stand by fore and aft.'

The quartermaster's voice was deep and resonant and he enunciated each word very clearly into the ship's loud-speaker. There was not a single nook or cranny aboard the *Free Enterprise* in which some sleepy passenger or member of the crew could escape from the forceful impact of his announcement; and the wind carried the message across the sea until it reverberated against the tall white cliffs and the granite jetties encircling the port of Dover.

It was three o'clock on a fine summer's afternoon and the ship rolled gently in the swell below the South Foreland Lighthouse, waiting for her signal to enter the harbour. There were soft grey cumulus clouds drifting slowly across the sky like a flock of indolent sheep, and the sea was an ever-changing kaleidoscope of emeralds, sapphires and amethysts; a heaving shimmering mass of water borne on the restless tide, with here and there a diamond bracelet sparkling in the sunshine along the crest of some gallivanting wave.

I was busy adding up columns of figures and filling in the final details on the cargo manifest when the call to action came; but I had known at least five minutes beforehand exactly where we were by the feel of the ship under my feet and the general commotion outside the purser's office. I glanced at Muriel out of the corner of my right eye and she smiled briefly and said; 'All right, you can go if you want to, but don't be late down on the car-deck this time for there are 597 landing-tickets to collect!'

I ran out on to the top deck and took several deep sniffs of pure salt air while I watched a cluster of hungry seagulls hovering above the galley door at the after end of the ship. The starboard rail was lined with wide-eyed passengers jostling each other for a front line view of England, which many of them were gazing at for the first time in their lives.

'*Mira el faro blanco!*' exclaimed a Spanish woman ecstatically, pointing a plump forefinger at the lighthouse up on the cliffs. '*Qué precioso! Qué sitio maravilloso!*'

She swung round to make sure that her husband was in the best position to profit from the beauty of his surroundings, and when I saw the expression of rapture on her face I felt a warm sensation of pride and pleasure and it seemed as if I was looking at my special corner of England for the first time, through a foreigner's eyes. Sometimes it happened two or three times in the same day, but I always wanted to rush forward and shout at them—'You're quite right, it *is* the most marvellous spot in the whole world! And have you noticed that white house with the green roof up on the cliffs very close to the lighthouse? Well that's where I live . . .'

Sometimes I managed to restrain myself, and on that particular afternoon my attention was soon diverted by Snowy who was urgently beckoning to me from the poop. I climbed up the iron ladder and he seized my left elbow and pulled me towards the stern-rail. By this time the ship had passed through the eastern entrance of Dover Harbour and was beginning to swing round preparatory to moving astern into her berth in the Camber.

'D'you see that navy-blue speck moving about up there on the cliff-face?' demanded Snowy, pointing dramatically towards the great chalk cliffs which towered above the car-ferry berths.

'Yes, of course I can!' I lied cheerfully, for I had no intention of letting him know that I could hardly see anything beyond the flagstaff on the stern without my spectacles.

'Well, there's something very odd about it,' he continued, warming to his subject. 'First of all it's been there in exactly the same place, just by the groove in the chalk that looks like a W, at the same time every afternoon this week. And today, unless

I'm much mistaken, it's flying a piece of red bunting from its yard-arm!'

'You don't say!' I exclaimed, doing my best to assume an expression of innocent surprise. 'How clever you are to pick out details like that, Snowy, with all the other thousands of specks up there on that cliff-face. I'll have to run or Muriel will be shouting for me down on the car-deck. Let me know if it's there again tomorrow?'

Snowy's seafaring eyes, which were renowned for picking up some remote mountain summit or the outline of a mangrove plantation a great many miles away on the distant horizon, began to twinkle as they turned away from the shore. I swung round quickly and made a dive for the iron ladder, and as soon as he was out of sight I began to sing *There'll be blue birds over, the white cliffs of Dover* . . . at the top of my voice. A few of the passengers looked rather startled and Charlie Walker, who was on speaking terms with me again, made a great pantomime of blocking up his ears with plugs as he sped by. But there were seagulls singing in the sky above me and the clouds had just parted to allow a golden shaft of sunlight through; and it had settled on the upper half of the cliffs directly behind the Camber.

* * * * *

Dick's job as a locum at St Margaret's Bay came to an end about the same time as our two weeks of day duty, and he drove over to Ashford one morning to have an interview for a permanent job as a G.P. in that neighbourhood. The suspense was almost unbearable as I realized that he might be compelled to work in some remote part of the British Isles if he was not successful at the interview. However, I need not have worried; he came to fetch me at the Eastern Docks that night with a broad grin on his face and the news that he had been invited to become a third partner in the Ashford practice, starting from September 1st.

The mid-August week of nights was exceptionally hard work. On most crossings the ship was crammed full of cars and passengers, and many of the crew looked worn out and jaded, and much in need of a good holiday. The drinking became heavier as an antidote to the long working hours and lack of sleep, and sometimes we had the strange sensation of losing our sense of awareness and becoming obsessed with the idea of sleep; just to be able to go home and stay in bed for days and days and days on end ... However, I often noticed that the whole ship's company seemed to breathe a sigh of relief as soon as the ship left harbour. The cool night air smelt of seaweed and salt water, and sometimes I noticed a faint whiff of wood-smoke drifting out to sea from some cosy hearth behind the brow of the cliffs.

One stormy night that week there were fewer passengers than usual on the return voyage from Calais to Dover, so Muriel left me in charge of the office while she had a short rest. It was one of those sorts of nights when everything movable was vigorously on the move. Two biros, the franking-machine and a bundle of passenger tickets had already disappeared on to the floor of our office, and when a jar of pickled cucumbers which Muriel had bought for Billy Steer decided to follow them, I got down on to my hands and knees and began to grovel around under the desk in a brave attempt to recapture them. At that moment a distinguished-looking old gentleman wearing fluffy grey sideboards and a monocle in his left eye leant right over the desk and, addressing me as '*Chère Madame*', he implored me to lead him with the utmost haste to the cabin he had reserved, as the sea was too agitated for Madame la Baronne and she desired the privacy that only a cabin could afford.

We had only two passenger's cabins on the *Free Enterprise*, and they were so seldom used that one tended to forget their existence. I searched through Muriel's lists and saw that a Baron de Montrachet-Villeneuve from Paris had booked Cabin A for the 0130 crossing, and there was a hastily scribbled note from Mr Briggs to say that he was to be treated with the utmost civility! By this time I was no longer underneath the desk, and having dusted off my skirt and stockings and found the appropriate key, I offered to lead him down to the cabin. On a bench nearby Madame la Baronne, who the old gentleman addressed as '*Ma pauvre Chiffon!*', sat huddled inside an ocelot coat with a ranch mink collar, looking very grumpy and introspective.

We descended the heaving stairs to the lower deck in a manner which lacked some of the grace and dignity I felt the occasion demanded. However, Cabin A was facing us at the bottom of the staircase and, fitting the key into the lock, I threw open the door with a grand gesture and said '*Voilà!* ...' Suddenly my mouth went dry and I could not think of anything further to add; for I had just switched on the light and noticed that the bed was already occupied by a man and a woman who were very scantily attired and seemed to be quite unaware of our presence!

* * * * *

'The peak period congestion,' as Mr Briggs from the Dover office described it, was also the period for some of the seamen to pick quarrels with the stewards and passengers. There had to be some scapegoat when the pressures were building up and they felt an urgent need to relieve their pent-up feelings ...

'Ruddy passengers are the whole cause of the trouble—worst type of cargo you can carry on any ship!' growled Dapper, who was suffering from a monumental hang-over. 'If it wasn't for them we wouldn't need all these lousy stewards fluffing around with their fancy manners and posh voices!'

Unlike most of the crew, Dapper had no home of his own to go to when he came off duty, so he lived in the Seamen's Mission in Snargate Street. He was like a throw-back to the sailors with pigtails who sang rousing sea-shanties as they manned the capstan on some mighty square-rigged sailing ship. His voice was loud and raucous, and of the right timbre to carry from the skysail yards to the deck in a gale; but there were times when he took a dislike to humanity in general and certain classes of people in particular; and Dapper never saw any good reason to conceal his feelings.

A few days after his outburst about the passengers and stewards, Dapper was given the sack. It appeared that he had described a female motorist in a beaver-lamb driving-jacket, who was unable to start the engine of her car, as 'that effing old fur bag who doesn't know the front end of a car from its arse!'

Unbeknown to our Geordie seaman, she was an influential person with very acute hearing. As soon as she touched land she wrote a tempestuous letter to the Directors of Townsend Ferries Ltd., and two days later we found ourselves attending Dapper's farewell party in Charlie Walker's cabin. Of all his friends, the

Ancient Mariner was the one who felt most bitterly about his dismissal, as he shared the same sentiments as the unhappy seaman about the type of cargo we were carrying.

'We've had our holds filled with just about everything from coal to grain, sand, cement, live sheep, timber and pig's manure on the ships I've served in,' exclaimed the A.M., with a gleam of nostalgia illuminating his angry blue eyes. 'And believe me there isn't one of those cargoes I wouldn't rather have than this unspeakable load of sewage.'

Over in Calais there were similar signs of stress among our friends the dock policemen. They were compelled to work for incredibly long hours by English standards, and to grapple with double the usual number of difficult passengers as well as the daily cargo of British drunks from *The Queen of the Channel.* Pierrot looked hollow-eyed and ill, but in between the arrival of two coach parties he informed me quite casually that his grandfather was a Jugoslav from some remote village in the mountains of Montenegro. As soon as his attention was engaged elsewhere I moved across to where his *copain*, Raphael, was standing and asked; 'Why did Pierrot never tell me before that he had Jugoslav blood in him? He knows that it is one of my favourite countries.'

'*Exactement!* That is what he had figured to himself. Believe me there is no more Jugoslav blood circulating through his veins than there is Pernod in a honey-pot!'

* * * * *

I had invited my mother to stay for a few days in the latter half of August, and her visit coincided with Dick's return to Kent after spending two weeks at home with his father. My mother's arrival was timed to occur during the late afternoon of the day I finished night duty, and I had visualized being able to have at least six hours in bed before her car appeared over the crest of the hill. As luck would have it we were late coming off duty that morning, and I had promised to give the Captain a lift home and drop Charlie Walker at the Kingsdown Golf Club. All went well to begin with; I drove to Robin Hatch where the Captain began to disembark, but he and Charlie were in the middle of a fascinating discussion about which was the strongest motivating force in a man's life—sex or survival. We each had thoughts we wished to air on the subject, so we climbed out of the car and stood in the middle of the road raising our voices to be heard above the general clamour and heat of argument; and then a green Hillman Hunter drove silently into our midst, and there was my mother and her companion, both wearing 'just the sort of thing I expected from that dreadful ship' expressions on their faces!

That rather difficult moment set the tone for the next few days. I had made some tentative arrangements with Dick that we would meet him for lunch on Wednesday at an inn called the White Horse, in the picturesque village of Chilham. It turned out to be a morning of blinding sunshine, with the temperature about 90° Fahrenheit and a white heat haze hovering above the parched and languid fields. The Ford Popular boiled up once or twice on the main road to Canterbury and my mother said; 'I do wish we'd come in my car as I suggested. You really must get hold of something decent to drive later on this autumn!'

Eventually we drove into Chilham with Mother fanning herself rather pointedly with the latest edition of *Reader's Digest*, and beads of sweat pouring down the back of my neck. I caught a fleeting glimpse of Dick standing on the corner near the White Horse, and suddenly I realized that he was suffering even more than I was that morning! As if she could read my thoughts, my mother asked; 'Who is that very nervous-looking young man with the greenish face standing near the entrance to the inn?'

A few minutes later the introductions had been made and Mother led the way into the dining-room of the White Horse where she ordered a substantial luncheon for three. All her life she has been an excellent trencher-woman and she tends to judge people by their appetites, so she was deeply disturbed to find that Dick merely picked at his food and could hardly swallow more than a few mouthfuls.

'You really ought to see a doctor!' she exclaimed, quite forgetting that he was one, after her third unsuccessful attempt to give him another helping of steak and kidney pudding.

Dick tried to explain that the intense heat had made him feel off colour; but each time he relapsed into an oppressive silence my mother became more talkative and expansive than usual, prattling on about one thing and another to keep the ball rolling, as she explained to me later. Dick nodded politely from time to time, and the temperature steadily rose into the middle nineties.

'Please God let this end soon!' I prayed on the other side of the table.

He must have heard my prayer for He sent the waiter along to remove the last remnants of our roly-poly pudding and to ask if we would prefer our coffee to be served in the dining-room or the lounge.

'No coffee!' we cried with one accord, and my mother began to fan Dick with her *Reader's Digest* while she waited for the bill.

The remainder of her visit passed without a hitch and I even thought that I detected a glimmer of approval in her eyes when she said goodbye and drove away on her journey north, a few days later.

* * * * *

I went to work in the dark one Sunday night in September. The sun had already set behind the black silhouette of the castle and low banks of stratus clouds were rushing towards me from the west. Suddenly I realized that the summer was nearly over; the most beautiful summer I had ever known. And because the days were swiftly drawing in and the nights extending themselves, I wanted to clutch at every sunbeam and arrest its progress; and make the month of September last for ever and ever.

Most of the crew had begun to feel like rational human beings again now that the busiest part of the summer season had come to an end; there was time to chatter and laugh and eat proper meals, and to make plans for their holidays which would be starting in a month's time. The conversation often turned to the wide-spread rumours about a new ship already on the stocks over in Rotterdam; a sister-ship to the *Free Enterprise* which might be launched the following spring. Townsend Ferries Ltd. had always been a one-ship company, and the emotions stirred by these rumours were vigorous and diverse.

'It won't never be the same no more!' declared one seaman gloomily. 'When you come to think about it, we've always bin like one big family, see what I mean?'

I saw what he meant all too clearly, and felt sad and depressed when I thought of the effect it would have on such a close-knit and contented ship's company; for I knew that once the syndicate from Coventry had really got into their stride, Captain Townsend's splendid little shipping company would be a thing of the past.

* * * * *

On the third morning that week our dawn broke near the whistle buoy on the Riden de Calais. There were dark wispy clouds floating across a gentle pink and green sky, and all the Calais harbour lights were soft and dewy-eyed, beckoning us back to France. Then the sun rose bright and strong, and the roofs of the wagons-lits on the Orient Express shone like polished silver under their carpet of early morning dew; and even the old black cranes lifted up their heads as if they were about to sing a triumphant serenade to the dawn sky.

Muriel and I went ashore together after we had collected all the landing-tickets. We exchanged the usual greetings with the Calais mooring-party, then I noticed Pierrot standing outside the custom-house, a different Pierrot to the one I had known for the past few months. His shoulders drooped, there were dark rings under his eyes and an aura of hopeless despondency hung about him so that even Raphael seemed to be avoiding him.

'Cheer up, Sunshine!' Muriel exclaimed, as she hurried towards Billy Steer's office. 'You look as if you've backed the wrong horse?'

Pierrot showed no signs of having understood her, but he put out an arm to prevent me from following and announced in a sepulchral whisper that he was being transferred to Lille next day and might never see us again; before I had a chance to probe into the matter any further Muriel returned and swept me away. There was a long line of cars waiting to embark on the *Free Enterprise*, and we did not finish loading until a few minutes before the ship was due to sail. Just as the last car disappeared down the ramp and we were about to follow it, Pierrot ran out of the custom-house and embraced each of us in turn with a fervour which astonished the Calais mooring-party and Charlie Walker, who was superintending the remnants of the embarkation.

'You will come to visit me occasionally in Lille, *n'est-ce-pas*?' His voice sounded hollow and disembodied against the rumbling machinery of the stern door closing. The ship began to move astern and Muriel's reassuring answer was lost in the wind of our departure.

The following night was rough and stormy. The south cone, predicting a southerly gale within the next few hours, had been hoisted on the signal station mast in Dover; and as soon as we drew clear of the harbour entrance the ship began to plunge into a welter of huge waves with foaming white crests. They reared up out of the darkness and crashed against the hull with an impact which made the whole ship shudder and creak from stem to stern. I stood on the shelter deck watching for a few minutes and it seemed to me, as it had so often done before, that our ship was a live creature and not just a mass of steel frames and plates welded together; and she was struggling valiantly for survival amid primeval forces which could never be controlled or tamed by man.

Muriel and I landed together in Calais at midnight, and as soon as we reached the custom-house we noticed Raphael standing inside talking to a new policeman, a stocky red-faced man who wore a close-cropped military moustache. We went across to them, and after the introductions had been made Muriel mentioned to Raphael that she hoped Pierrot would settle happily in his new posting at Lille, as he had seemed very upset about it the previous night.

'He has no new posting—*merde, non*!' he replied, with a look of surprise which momentarily softened his hard brown eyes. 'Doubtless you have observed that he has been somewhat indisposed during the past few weeks? Finally I persuaded him to seek the advice of a doctor, and it appears that he has contracted an acute form of pulmonary tuberculosis. This morning he went to the big hospital in Lille and it is said that he will never work in the police force again.'

The three of us stood together in silence for a few moments, in remembrance of our absent friend; and high above us a sleepy midnight pigeon rustled its feathers in sympathy among the rafters which supported the roof of the custom-house. Presently Monsieur Delanghe strode towards us and announced that there was an unexpected coach-load of school teachers from Milan waiting to board the ship, and would we encourage them to embark as soon as possible as two of them were making *bêtises* in the foyer of his office. The spell was broken and Raphael returned to his post while Muriel and I prepared to intercept the party of Italians.

The wind dropped and the sea calmed down at the turn of the tide. The *Free Enterprise* was returning to Dover on our last crossing, and as we approached the English coast I could see a light mist swirling across the upper layers of the cliffs. They seemed a thousand miles high and a thousand miles wide for there were no horizons or summits or outlines of any kind that morning. And the world around us was painted in pastel shades of pink, mauve and blue, the soft translucent colours of the moonstone. It was a scene of marvellous serenity, and into the middle of it motored a small wooden fishing-vessel called *Golden Harvester*. Her skipper wore a green knitted scarf wrapped tightly round his neck and tucked into the collar of his oilskin jacket, and I saw him wave to our Captain as his boat rolled dramatically in the wash of our passing.

* * * * *

Dick had just begun his new job as a G.P. in Ashford, and we decided to celebrate by having a house-warming supper. He had managed to find a small furnished flat in the town, and the day that he moved in we prepared a special banquet of smoked salmon, grilled steaks with baked potatoes and salad, lychees for me and cheese for Dick, and a bottle of champagne with which to toast the success of his new job. He had lit a log fire in the sitting-room, and I well remember how cosy it all looked and how reluctant I was to go on duty that evening.

Shortly after sunrise next morning I was lingering on the top deck on my way back from the Radio Office when I noticed a little black tramp steamer on our starboard bow, steaming slowly across our course under a vast umbrella of black smoke. That ancient puffer was dwarfed by the volume of soot pouring out of her tall thin funnel, and there was something so endearing about her appearance that I sat down on a liferaft to watch her.

'It's not often you see an old-fashioned tramp steamer like that one nowadays, is it?' I remarked to Charlie Walker who was leaning over the ship's rail nearby.

'It certainly isn't,' he laughed. 'She's a genuine museum piece and I believe the A.M.'s as happy as a sandboy on her!'

'The A.M.?' I asked in some astonishment. At that moment a thin reedy noise issued from the little steamer's siren and a familiar figure appeared on her rickety bridge, waving a blue and yellow striped bath-towel.

'Yes, that's the A.M. himself!' shouted Charlie, as we waved and jumped up and down to attract his attention. 'You must have been off duty when all the trouble brewed up,' he continued. 'We'd had a pig of a night on watch, and then some silly cow of a passenger caused him the maximum amount of aggra. and he just couldn't take it any longer—you know how he's always felt about human cargoes—well it took him three or four minutes to tell her exactly what he thought of her! So there he is on his new ship which has something to do with the Channel Tunnel lark, and they say she was a boom defence vessel in the last war.'

'What's her name?' I asked him as I turned to go below.

'The *Fair Barbette*,' replied Charlie, to my intense surprise.

* * * * *

The autumn equinox came and went, and scarcely a day passed without a distant glimpse of that tall black umbrella under which we knew that the brave little tramp steamer was ploughing her way to and fro across the stormy strait.

A few days later September faded out in a soft grey mist, and A Watch started night duty again; four nights at sea and then it was our last duty watch of all before the ship went back on to her winter schedule, and the extra crews were signed off. There was a touch of frost in the air that night and the full moon rose majestically into the starry heavens. I had decided to walk across the cliffs to work, and the rest of A Watch were already waiting at the top of the ramp to board the ship when I joined them after my long hike. They were all there—the Captain, Ian Perriam, Charlie Walker, old Mr Boys, Narvik, Snowy,

Muriel, Eveline, Jonesy and all the others. I found that I was staring at each of them in turn, to try and fix them in my memory for ever and ever.

That brilliant cold October night was like a stage setting for some pitiless drama; but there was also an illusory impression of normality about the whole scene. We left Dover at 10.30 p.m. as usual, and somewhere near the South Goodwin Lightvessel Jack came rushing into our office on Captain's rounds.

'What are your plans for the next few weeks?' he asked us, although I suspected that he knew the answers perfectly well.

Muriel was all right because she would be back on the ship again after a month's leave, but I felt strangely insecure and on the verge of tears. When I told him that I would be returning to London very soon, he grunted sympathetically and said I must come across and visit Miriam and him whenever I came down to St Margaret's Bay at the week-ends. The news had just come through that Jack was to take command of the new ship, *Free Enterprise II*, when she was launched over in Holland the following summer. Everyone was very pleased about this, and most of the permanent crew were hoping to accompany him to his new command. Little did they foresee that he would be moving one rung higher up the ladder every year until, finally, he became Commodore of Townsend's vast fleet of car-ferries.

The Captain moved on to the Snack Bar, and I noticed that Jonesy was entertaining a group of passengers to a particularly noisy rendering of *When the Red, Red Robin* . . .

Muriel and I both landed in Calais at midnight. We shook hands warmly with all the Calais mooring-party who expressed their desolation at the thought of not seeing us again for a long while. Old Billy Steer, wearing his customary brown Trilby hat, was waiting at the top of the ramp with a little pot of African violets to present to Muriel. Ives and Lèon were on duty at the entrance to the custom-house, and Monsieur Delanghe soon appeared with a harassed expression on his face and told us that there were some *sales Suisses* in a large Dormobile who were attempting to cross to Dover without paying their fares.

I felt numb and detached during the first loading in Calais, as if I was observing it all through binoculars from a long distance away. There were two caravans, a Morris 1,000, an old Bugatti and one or two other cars, all returning to England after late holidays in the south. Above us a sleeping-car of the Orient Express reposed under the brilliant silver moon, and the attendant shouted hoarse obscenities at one of the Calais porters who had just urinated against the side of the carriage farther down the line.

Muriel and I had been too busy to notice much of what was happening around us during the first half of the night; I believe it was sometime after our second departure from Dover that it began to dawn on us that some of the crew had been celebrating the end of the summer season ever since our first departure the previous night. My own head felt as if a choir of grasshoppers was singing inside it, and even Muriel made a muddle of the cargo manifest by stating that there were four motor-bycles, two with slide-cars, about to land in France!

After the moon set it became colder than ever, and the sun did not rise during our second visit to Calais as the sky was shrouded in heavy purple clouds. I could just make out the lighthouse on the Walde Sands and the church spire at Gravelines in the wintry dawn light.

A man in a pillar-box red sport's car drove flashily off the ship in Calais; as he passed me he raised his deer-stalker and called out cheerily; 'The best of British luck to you, darling!'

'I dare say I shall need it from now onwards,' I muttered to myself in a fit of self-pity, as I trudged up the ramp carrying the Calais Bag over one shoulder.

Billy Steer came to say goodbye, then Monsieur Delanghe and Ives and Lèon, and finally all the Calais mooring-party, one by one. The baker had brought us fifty long thin loaves, and Reg Stedman helped me to carry them aboard as very few of the crew had landed that morning. At last the stern door was closed and I could feel the great engines vibrating under my feet as the ship began to move astern. I paused on the shelter deck on my way back to the office to watch a fisherman raising his square net at the far end of the western jetty. A whiff of Gaulloise tabacco drifted across the sleeping harbour, and then the ship sped past the two small lighthouses guarding the entrance and I said goodbye to France.

A scene of uninhibited revelry greeted me back on the lounge-deck. Most of the crew, apart from the duty quartermaster and engineer and one or two greasers, were gathered round the bars and they were all busily engaged treating each other to the final rounds of alcoholic refreshments, blowing trumpets and small foghorns, dancing on the tops of the bars and some of the tables, and one man was standing on his head in front of the shop. A few astonished passengers were huddled together in the far corner of the lounge, but it was clear that the ship belonged to us that night and each member of the crew was intent on expressing his feelings in the way which appealed to him most.

Some while later Muriel ordered two large glasses of brandy and ginger ale—'To pull us together before docking in Dover,' as she so aptly put it. We had just started singing *There'll be blue birds over, the white cliffs of Dover* ... when the quartermaster's voice came booming over the loud-speaker; 'Harbour Stations, Harbour Stations; Stand by fore and aft.'

I ran out on deck under the sombre grey canopy of the English dawn. The *Fair Barbette* had just come out of harbour with her black umbrella raised above her funnel, and some fat Dover seagulls were hovering near the entrance to the galley. A French day-tripper squeezed the arm of his fiancée and implored her to regard the white lighthouse on top of the cliffs. 'Was it not *fantastic*!' he demanded.

'That's where I live up there, between the two lighthouses,' I began to tell them, then I turned away because my eyelids felt moist and prickly ... perhaps it was just the cold sea air; but suddenly I wanted to climb into one of the lifeboats and hide there for hours and hours.

The Shipping Master and the men from the Seamen's and Merchant Navy Officer's Unions came aboard as soon as the ship had settled into her berth. Muriel sat behind a desk next to the Shipping Master, wearing her official face and talking in a dull monotone about insurance coding and who to contact at the Labour Exchange. Half an hour later all the extra crew members and I were signed off, and we changed into our ordinary clothes and ran down the companionway to the car-deck for the last time.

The East Cliff towered gaunt and grey above the car-ferry

terminal, and the hungry morning gulls were shouting to each other high above me on the cliff-face. I could just make out a white Mini parked close to the check point at the entrance to the Eastern Docks. I began to run towards it as fast as my legs would carry me...

* * * * *

The twenty-third of June was a day of brilliant shafts of sunlight darting in and out among huge cauliflower clouds; the north-west wind blew hard and gusty, and the clouds raced each other triumphantly across the sapphire-blue sky.

The garden round the old lighthouse was in the full flush of its midsummer glory. There was a solid carpet of tiny flowers—scarlet pimpernels, forget-me-nots, germander speedwells, buttercups and daisies... literally hundreds and thousands of daisies—and in among them the taller flowers, the marsh marigolds, red valerian, dog roses and moon-daisies raised their proud heads like topsail schooners sailing through a crowded anchorage. I wondered whether the Elysian Fields looked like that as I bent down to take off my smart white shoes; they had high stiletto heels which would cause havoc among the tiny plants.

The garden was full of people as well as flowers that afternoon. First of all there was Dick and me—well, we were the principal actors on the stage as we had just been married—and there was Dick's father wearing a red carnation in his buttonhole, and my mother smiling serenely under a white straw hat which had a large camellia attached to the brim. Then there was Dick's brother and sister-in-law, and his uncle and three aunts; and my one aunt and a few other close relations and very best friends on both sides, including some from St Margaret's Bay and the *Free Enterprise*.

When we returned from the church there was champagne and a great deal of food—my mother had seen to that—but the only thing I can clearly recall is a magnificent boar's head which Bonzo discovered before breakfast that morning, and would certainly have devoured if I had not come into the dining-room during his initial reconnaissance. He was dressed for the occasion with an enormous blue bow attached to his collar, but nothing could alter the bad-tempered and woebegone expression on his face.

Jack Dawson, who was not supposed to be there at all because it was his duty watch, rose to his feet and uttered a few stirring words; then Bobby Melhuish spoke, and finally Dick . . . I was not really listening to what they were saying, but I do remember thinking that it was the best party I had been to for a very long time!

After the cake, which had white sugared sailing-boats and car-ferries skimming across it, had been cut and the champagne had flowed for several hours, we suddenly found ourselves down by the old lighthouse; I believe it was Jack who suggested the move . . . Anyway there we all were with the dog chasing rabbits and the gulls shouting to each other in the sky above us. The sea was amethyst-mauve and lapis-lazuli blue, a shimmering surging miracle which reflected some of the splendour and majesty of the great scudding clouds.

Presently I glanced over one shoulder and noticed a pale green ferry-boat with two red funnels, side by side, heading out towards the coast of France. She blew five blasts on her siren as she sped past the South Foreland; and soon afterwards Dick and I ran through a whirlwind of confetti to his new car, a red Alfa Romeo, and we drove away over the crest of the hill with a bunch of tin cans and a very old sea-boot thumping up the rough road behind us.

12. THE ROAD TO THE STARS

'Now smile and nod your heads to show you've understood,' said Captain Coolen, hopefully surveying his class of twenty-six budding ocean navigators.

The man in the corduroy breeches tittered nervously, but the rest of us preserved a weighty silence, our expressions ranging between the total bewilderment of an imbecile and the jovial wiliness of a politician. We were nearing the end of our weekly evening class at the School of Navigation and our instructor had spent the past two hours showing us how to solve the PZX Triangle, an imaginary spherical triangle in the sky, by means of the Marcq St Hilaire method, using the spherical haversine formula; or, in plain language, how to manipulate a jumble of figures pulled at random from the Nautical Almanac and

Norie's Tables, combined with a few simple sextant shots of the sun, moon or stars and some chronometer readings, to calculate one's precise position, give or take a mile or two, in the middle of the ocean. It seemed to me the most wonderful and exciting concept I had ever listened to, but I had to admit that I had hardly understood a single word the whole evening!

Dick and I had come a long way in the pursuit of navigational knowledge since our voyage to Gravelines in the two Folkboats. First there had been the summer when he changed his job, with a glorious three months' interval between the end of one and the beginning of the next. We sailed *Martha* fifteen hundred miles northwards to the west coast of Norway, stopping at almost every harbour we passed on the way there; then we flew on to the Arctic Circle to spend a few days with our parents in the Lofoten Islands. It was a very beautiful, never-to-be-forgotten summer, but afterwards it was harder than ever to settle down to the humdrum routine of everyday life ashore.

When living aboard a Folkboat for any length of time, Dick had one recurrent complaint; there was nowhere inside the cabin with sufficient headroom for him to stand up straight to do up his trousers! During long spells of bad weather with wet clothing festooning the interior, it certainly *was* a rather cramped and bleak existence unless, like me, one was completely blind to all the boat's imperfections. But on lengthy sea passages even I had to concede that it was almost impossible to cook or sleep inside the cabin in any sort of rough weather, unless one had the constitution of a rhinoceros.

After much wavering and weighing things in the balance, and several more short voyages to the Continent in *Martha*, we decided to have a larger boat built for us and to persuade Noel Jordan to take back his much-loved Folkboat when our new vessel was launched the following spring. He had no sailing-yacht at that time as he had had two coronaries and been compelled to give up ocean racing. He was overjoyed with our proposals, and insisted on buying a third share in *Martha*'s ownership that same day.

Roskilde was designed by a friend of ours, John Russell, an intrepid seafarer from the west coast of Scotland; and she was built by the famous Scottish yard of McGruer's on the Gareloch.

A thirty-one foot, clinker-built cutter with larch planking on iroko frames, she was fashioned on the lines of the Shetland sixareens whose ancestry could be traced right back to the Viking cargo ships of Western Norway. She turned out to be a tough and beautiful ocean-voyager—the sort of boat in which you could sail round the world without any qualms.

During *Roskilde*'s maiden voyage from the Clyde to Dover, via the Caledonian Canal and the east coast, there were many Scottish fishermen who cast experienced eyes over her, then sagely nodded their heads and pronounced their approval. I shall always remember the old skipper in Macduff who sat on a bollard up above us, calmly smoking his pipe while he peered at our boat in a sort of trance; and suddenly he exclaimed, 'That's a bonny wee boat ye have doon there, Muster. Aye, she's chust sublime!'

* * * * *

Back in England nothing had gone according to plan. Some months before the launching of *Roskilde*, Dick and I realized that something was very wrong with little *Martha*. Each time we took her out sailing, even with Noel aboard, she behaved in the most extraordinary manner: the first time she split her mainsail from top to bottom, the second time she ran aground and on a third occasion her boom hit Dick a resounding blow causing him to fall on to a sharp stake, as a result of which he had to have eight stitches in his leg. Despite all those ominous signs, I began to feel more and more depressed at the thought of parting with her. However marvellous the new boat turned out to be, I just could not bear the thought of saying goodbye to my old friend.

Noel sailed *Martha* round to Burnham for laying up that winter. He made a splendid fast passage although he was battling against a strong east wind most of the way, and darkness overtook him before he reached the River Crouch. But it was a final challenge for him, a day of total dedication to the things he loved most. A few months later he had another coronary and died almost immediately.

Noel's widow, Ursula, asked us to take her out to sea in *Martha* to scatter his ashes over the waters where he had spent so many happy hours. Unexpectedly it turned out to be a golden afternoon of perfect tranquillity, and not an occasion for the shedding of tears. When we left him on that shining summer sea, we knew that the man who had brought so much sunshine and hope into the lives of all his friends would never be forgotten; and the standards of perfection upon which he insisted in all his sailing ventures would be a goal worth striving for in the future.

There had never been any question of selling *Martha* to a stranger, so Dick and I did some hard thinking to devise a scheme for keeping two wooden sailing-boats in good condition and usefully employed. He had five weeks holiday each year, and it was only natural that we should use *Roskilde* for our summer cruise and most week-end trips in the future. So what should we do with little *Martha*?

Dick had worked for several years as Deputy Medical Officer in the Borough of Newham, and become very friendly with the directors of Social Services there. And when our plans began to take shape, they bravely agreed to accept the risk of entrusting me with a few of their children living in Council Homes, 'in care', to teach them rowing and sailing and the rudiments of seamanship and navigation. About this time we noticed that *Martha* had ceased her extraordinary pranks; and her behaviour was quite exemplary from then onwards!

With this project in view and a larger boat to handle part of the time, we promptly enrolled at the School of Navigation for the Yachtmaster's Offshore Course. After six months under the brilliant tuition of Captain Ian McLaren, a charming Scottish sea captain with an Extra Master's Ticket, we managed to pass the two-hour oral examination and also the gruelling tests during a week at sea off the coast of Anglesey. Encouraged by this success and proudly flourishing our new certificates, we then embarked on the Ocean Yachtmaster's Course. But this proved so difficult that it took us two winters, covering the same ground twice, to pass the theoretical examination; and the practical one, out of sight of land, has yet to come.

The following summer we had the unusual and exciting

experience of finding our latitude off the west coast of Spitzbergen by taking a meridian altitude of the sun at midnight!

* * * * *

In the meantime Ursula, who had not wanted to part with Noel's share in the ownership of *Martha*, was helping me to teach eight little boys from a long-term home in Forest Gate. Their ages ranged from eight to thirteen, and their headmasters had agreed to let each of them off school for one afternoon a fortnight. Every Tuesday we met four of them at the London Marina, and after a picnic lunch on the boat we set off from Gallion's Reach, sailing up or downstream, according to the wind and tide.

For the first few weeks I had nightmares regularly every Monday night, wondering if I should lose one of the children overboard or we should have some fearful accident. But, miraculously, nothing like that happened and *Martha* got on well with her new crew and took care of them, and some of them grew to love her and think of her as their very own boat —something special in their lives which were grey and bleak in many other respects. In midwinter, when it was cold and wet or blowing a gale, we studied knots and splices, tidal problems, the Rule of the Road and some simple chartwork, and the boys learnt to row in our dinghy on the calm waters of the London Marina. And once a year Captain McLaren came to give them a short examination to keep them up to the mark.

Some of the children like it best when a strong wind is blowing and *Martha* is heeled far over with her lee deck awash; but one or two of them prefer the dark days of winter when we light the paraffin stove and lamps early, and crowd into the warm security of the cabin.

Sometimes we bring *Roskilde* up the river for the winter, and she takes the place of *Martha* for a few months, so that each boat can have a thorough overhaul at Frank Halls' Yard at Walton-on-the-Naze every second year. Fortunately the two boats get on well together on the rare occasions when they meet, and there seems to be no jealousy or friction between them!

Last summer the two eldest boys in our group, Peter and Philip, had their sixteenth birthdays and left the home in

Forest Gate. Peter won a five-year apprenticeship at Whisstock's Yard at Woodbridge, one of the finest builders of wooden boats on the East Coast. And Philip was accepted for the Merchant Navy—the only one out of twenty-four during the week that he went for his interview.

* * * * *

In the old days, when I was sailing around single-handed, I often wondered about how I should feel if I had to share the boat permanently with someone else. Now, after fourteen years and some fairly long and arduous voyages, I can safely say that single-handed sailing has absolutely nothing to offer compared with double-handed sailing with the right man!